ROUTLEDGE LIBRARY EDITIONS:
MONETARY ECONOMICS

Volume 1

THE TRADE BALANCE IN MONETARY GENERAL EQUILIBRIUM

THE TRADE BALANCE IN MONETARY GENERAL EQUILIBRIUM

KENNETH W. CLEMENTS

Routledge
Taylor & Francis Group

LONDON AND NEW YORK

First published in 1984 by Garland Publishing, Inc.

This edition first published in 2017
by Routledge
2 Park Square, Milton Park, Abingdon, Oxon OX14 4RN

and by Routledge
711 Third Avenue, New York, NY 10017

Routledge is an imprint of the Taylor & Francis Group, an informa business

British Library Cataloguing in Publication Data
A catalogue record for this book is available from the British Library

ISBN: 978-1-138-73264-3 (Set)
ISBN: 978-1-315-16457-1 (Set) (ebk)
ISBN: 978-1-138-63350-6 (Volume 1) (hbk)
ISBN: 978-1-315-20728-5 (Volume 1) (ebk)

Publisher's Note
The publisher has gone to great lengths to ensure the quality of this reprint but
points out that some imperfections in the original copies may be apparent.

Disclaimer
The publisher has made every effort to trace copyright holders and would welcome
correspondence from those they have been unable to trace.

The Trade Balance
in Monetary
General Equilibrium

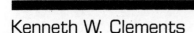

Kenneth W. Clements

Garland Publishing, Inc.
New York & London, 1984

Library of Congress Cataloging in Publication Data

Clements, Kenneth W., 1950–
    The trade balance in monetary general equilibrium.

    (Outstanding dissertations in economics)
    Originally published as the author's thesis, University of
Chicago, 1977.
    Bibliography: p.
    1. Balance of trade—Mathematical models. Equilibrium
(Economics) I. Title. II. Series.
HF1014.C56 1984   382.1'01'51   79-52688
ISBN 0-8240-4151-8

Printed in the United States of America

TABLE OF CONTENTS

ACKNOWLEDGMENTS

I have benefited from considerable guidance and support from my
thesis committee, Jacob A. Frenkel (Chairman), Harry G. Johnson,
Stephen P. Magee, and Larry A. Sjaastad.

I would also like to thank Clifford Wymer for many useful discus-
sions and for his generous help in establishing his computer programs on
the IBM 370/168 system at the University of Chicago. These programs were
used in all the computational work associated with this research, and are
referred to in detail in the text.

William Dougan, Peter Jonson and Nicholas Kiefer made useful comments on earlier drafts, which I would like to acknowledge. I would also
like to acknowledge a broad intellectual indebtedness to my old teacher,
Alan Powell.

My wife, Izan, supplied excellent research assistance, together
with help of a different nature.

Part of this research was completed at Monash University where I
was provided office space and for which I am grateful. I am also grateful
for the financial assistance provided by the Lilly Honor and Morganthau
Field Fellowships.

Altheia Chaballa typed the draft and Alyce Monroe the final version.
Both did a first-rate job, and, in addition, provided valuable editorial
assistance.

LIST OF ILLUSTRATIONS

LIST OF TABLES

CHAPTER I

INTRODUCTION

This dissertation is a contribution to applied international trade theory. We are concerned with the specification and estimation of a multi-sector general equilibrium model of the open economy. The model is formulated with the aim of assessing empirically the effects of three key policy variables on trade flows, domestic prices, and the trade balance. The policy variables with which we are concerned are the rate of growth of the stock of domestic credit, commercial policy, as represented by tariffs, and, finally, the exchange rate, which is taken to be pegged.

The model which is developed to analyze the effects of these policies builds on the general equilibrium models which are well-known from the pure theory of trade.[1] These are multisector models which have as their starting point a specification of technology and preferences. The supply side typically is characterized by a transformation function which, in turn, is related to the sectorial production functions and factor endowments. Domestic demand behavior is generally represented by a social utility function. The demand and supply sides are linked _via_ the budget constraint which requires that the value of income equal total expenditure. Taking the traded goods prices as parametric (the small country assumption), the trade flows in each commodity are identically the domestic excess supplies.

_____

[1]See, e.g., Johnson (1971) and Jones (1965).

1

All these features are in our model. In addition, however, we
draw a distinction between traded and nontraded goods.[1] Hence, while the
prices of the traded goods are exogenous, the nontraded goods prices are
determined endogenously within the model—they act to equate the domestic
supply of and demand for these commodities.

The model developed in this dissertation incorporates two key inno-
vations. Firstly, the movement to a position of long-run equilibrium is
not instantaneous, it takes time—i.e., the model is dynamic.[2] The
dynamics originate from the demand side of the model, and, in particular,
from the saving function. In its simplest form, the saving function which
we use states that saving is a constant fraction of the gap between the
long-run desired stock of wealth and the actual stock. In the long-run,
when desired and actual wealth are equal, saving ceases and income is
totally spent. This behavior is derived from an intertemporal utility
maximization problem which follows Dornbusch and Mussa (1975).

In this model, it turns out that wealth is the buffer stock to consumption so that if, for example, income falls unexpectedly, then, in the
short run, consumers decumulate wealth by spending more than their income
in order to smooth consumption. This decumulation does not represent a

---

[1]Recently, there has been considerable analysis of the role of nontraded goods in the pure theory of international trade [e.g., Komiya (1967)
and Melvin (1968)], as well as renewed interest in their role in the monetary aspects of trade [e.g., Dornbusch (1973)]; for an historical review of
the role of nontraded goods in balance of payments theory, see Arndt (1976)
and Oppenheimer (1974). It should, however, be pointed out that the recog-
nition of the traded/nontraded goods distinction goes back at least as far
as Ohlin (1933).

[2]We make no claim here of contributing a fundamental idea, viz.
dynamics in international trade theory. This is because dynamic models
have already appeared in the recent literature [e.g., Frenkel (1971) and
Fischer and Frenkel (1972, 1974a, 1974b)]. Our innovation here is much
more specific—that of analyzing the trade implications of a particular
saving theory.

position of long-run equilibrium, and it ceases once actual wealth falls
to the now lower desired stock of wealth; the desired stock falls because
income has fallen.[1]

Another property of our model of saving is that desired wealth and,
hence, also saving in the short-run are functions of relative prices. This
property generates a dynamic response to a tariff change, for example. The
qualitative response of saving to a relative price change cannot, it appears,
be given a sign a priori; it depends on the numerical values of certain
parameters and, hence, is an empirical issue.[2]

Since we are working with a general equilibrium model in which the
budget constraint is satisfied, it follows that the trade balance equals
both the difference between income and expenditure, and also the value of
exports less the value of imports. Hence, a trade balance surplus, for
example, implies that there is an excess flow demand for wealth, and this
is equal to the sum of the deficits on the capital and money accounts in
the balance of payments. The excess flow demand for wealth is matched by
an identical excess flow supply of commodities, so that Walras' Law holds.

In this dissertation, we have no portfolio theory and wealth is a
scalar. In turn, this means that we have no theory of the determination
of the balance of either the capital or the money accounts; we have a theory
only of the determination of their sum, which is the negative of the trade
balance. The reason for using scalar wealth, and hence, ruling out com-
positional effects is one of focus: we are interested in the determination

---

[1]Rodriguez (1976) develops an interesting related model which
possesses similar dynamic properties.

[2]The effect of relative prices on saving behavior has been previously analyzed by Harberger (1950). For a summary of subsequent develop-
ments along these lines, see Johnson (1956). It is of interest to note
that other more recent work in applied demand analysis also contains a
similar effect: see Lluch (1973).

of the trade balance and not in the division between the capital account and the money account.

The second, and perhaps more important, innovation of the model is the incorporation of monetary factors. An increase in the rate of growth of the money supply, or, more accurately, an increase in the rate of growth of domestic credit (since, with a fixed exchange rate, the monetary authority can only control the latter quantity) increases disposable income directly in our model. This is because it is assumed that this type of new money gets into the system via direct transfers. This helicopter-drop-type treatment can be justified in a number of ways, some of which are given later in the next chapter.

With this specification of income, domestic credit policy is a parameter of all demand curves in the sense that an expansionary credit policy causes all demand curves to shift up and to the right (if all goods are normal). Hence, other things equal, such a credit policy will have real effects from the demand side if supply curves are not all vertical. These effects can, however, only be nonzero in the short run. This is because, in the long run, the rate of growth of domestic credit cannot be arbitrarily chosen by the domestic monetary authority; i.e., these can only be short-run effects because the policy itself can only be maintained in the short-run. In the long-run, in order not to decumulate or accumulate international reserves indefinitely, the rate of growth of domestic credit in a small open economy with a fixed exchange rate must equal the rate of inflation in the rest of the world, adjusted for domestic growth.

We now give some more specific details of the structure of the model. The theoretical work is all aimed at producing a model which can be estimated with actual data. The usual lack of high quality time series data, i.e., the lack of sufficient independent variation in the explanatory variables, means that it is necessary to impose a good deal of specific structure on the data. By specific structure is meant a somewhat rigid specification of preferences and technology, in addition to utility and profit maximization, as maintained hypotheses. These types of restrictions are necessary for it to be possible to estimate simultaneously the own- and cross-price responses in a multisector general equilibrium framework.

The social utility function is assumed to be of the Klein-Rubin (1947) form. This utility function is directly additive, which means that the marginal rate of substitution between two commodities is a function only of the consumption of those goods. This implies that only a limited amount of substitution is allowed to take place. The solution to the intertemporal consumer problem determines how much of income is consumed. That is, we derive a consumption function, and this determines total expenditure on consumption. This quantity is then used in the atemporal problem of allocating the budget to the individual commodities; using the Klein-Rubin utility function, this yields Stone's (1954) linear expenditure system as the domestic demand equations.

We consolidate the government sector in with the private sector, so that the only other type of demand in the model, in addition to the consumer demands, is investment demand. For simplicity, all investment demands are taken as exogenous. The total domestic demand for a given commodity is the sum of the quantity demanded by consumers and investors.

On the supply side, we generate a system of supply equations by solving a producer maximization problem. Producers choose the composition of output to maximize its value subject to a transformation function. It is assumed that the transformation function is a quadratic form in the quantities produced by each sector.

The relationship between the supply side and the demand side of the model is as follows. The system of supply equations determines the quantity of each commodity supplied domestically. The inner product of this vector with the domestic price vector yields the value of output, and this is added to changes in domestic credit to yield nominal income. Income is then related to total consumption expenditure _via_ the consumption function, and the latter quantity drives the demand system.

Given the parametric prices of traded goods, the nontraded goods price adjusts to equate domestic demand and supply, so that the domestic excess supply for these is zero. The resulting equilibrium relative price of traded to nontraded goods is associated with the equilibrium excess supplies for the various traded commodities. Those goods with a negative excess domestic supply are imported, while the positive excess supplies determine exports.

The parameters of the model are then all estimated simultaneously by full information maximum likelihood. Annual post-war U.S. data are used in estimation; the whole economy is partitioned into three sectors which produce exportables, importables and nontraded goods. This empirical work is itself an advancement in applied econometrics because it represents the first time that a system of classical demand equations is estimated simultaneously with a complete set of supply equations.

The plan of the dissertation is as follows. The model is developed in Chapter II. In Chapter III, we set out the way in which the theoretical model is empirically applied, give the stochastic specification, discuss the estimation procedures, provide an overview of the data base, and then give the parameter estimates. Also, in that chapter, we simulate the model over the sample period. The estimated model is used in three applications

in Chapter IV: here, we simulate the effects of a devaluation of the U.S.
dollar, the imposition of a tariff on imports, and an expansionary domestic
credit policy. A summary and some concluding comments are given in
Chapter V. The U.S. data base, used to estimate the model, is described
and listed in the appendix.

CHAPTER II

THE MODEL

Introduction

In this chapter, we develop a simple multisector general equilibrium model of the open economy. The model is made up of a system of domestic demand equations, a consumption function, a wealth identity, a system of domestic supply equations, and finally, an income identity, which links the production side of the economy with the demand side.

For the demand side of the model, we set up an intertemporal utility maximization consumption problem. The solution determines both the amount of income which is spent on consumption, and the allocation of that expenditure to the individual commodities. An explicit functional form is used for the instantaneous utility function, and thus, together with intertemporal additivity of the utility functional, yield a consumption function and a system of demand equations in closed form.[1] The derivation of the consumption function closely follows Dornbusch and Mussa (1975).

On the supply side, we derive a system of supply equations from a producer maximization problem. Producers choose the composition of domestic output to maximize its value subject to technological constraints, and prices which each producer individually treats as parametric. We

---

[1]Some of the relevant literature on intertemporal consumption models in applied demand analysis is Betancourt (1973), Dixon and Lluch (1975), Klijn (1974), Lluch (1973), Philips (1974, Chap. X), and Powell (1974b, Chap. VI; 1974a).

characterize technology by assuming a particular functional form for the transformation function, which describes the ease with which the resources used to make one type of product can be used to make another.[1]

The motivation for deriving all the behavioral equations (which become the estimating equations) from maximization problems, rather than just writing them down in a form which can be conveniently analyzed and estimated, is twofold. First, this is a convenient way of automatically imposing the general restrictions on the demand and supply systems which come from economic theory. These are the restrictions of homogeneity of degree zero in all nominal variables, of symmetry of the price response matrix (compensated price response matrix for the demand equations), and finally, that the consumption point must satisfy the budget constraint, while the production point must lie on the transformation surface. Our behavioral equations satisfy all these restrictions. These restrictions are general in that they do not require any explicit functional forms.

The second reason for using this maximization framework is related to the empirical implementation of the model, and was referred to in Chapter I. To estimate the model, we use a relatively small number of time series observations. In addition, time series data typically have a low informational content due to common trends, etc. This all means that it is not possible to estimate price and income responses in a multisector framework in an unrestricted fashion. Hence, we impose some structure on these responses by using explicit functional forms for the social utility function and the transformation function. In particular, this structure is

---

[1]Some of the relevant more applied literature on transformation functions/multiple output production functions is Christensen, Jorgenson and Lau (1973), Diewert (1973, 1974), Dixon, Vincent and Powell (1976), Hall (1973), Hasenkamp (1976a, 1976b), Mundlak (1963, 1964), and Powell and Gruen (1968).

imposed by using functional forms which allow only a limited amount of substitution to take place.[1] This is a cost which has to be incurred to be able to estimate simultaneously all the parameters of a multisector model.

The production and consumption parts of the model are linked by an income definition, and it is here that money enters the system. It is assumed that increases in the domestic credit component of high-powered money get into the system via direct transfers, and, hence, raises income directly. This is the open economy analogue of the Sidrauski (1967) definition of income. As a result, in the simplest case of zero inflation, nominal income is identically equal to the sum of the value of output and the rate of increase in the domestic credit component of the monetary base.

To introduce the model in as simple a form as possible, in this chapter we abstract from two real world complications. First, that part of output devoted to investment in real capital is assumed to be zero. Second, we abstract from government spending and taxation--the only agents in the economy are consumers and producers. These two simplifications mean that output can only be either consumed domestically or exported. We dis- cuss in the next chapter the way in which we deal with these complications in the empirical implementation of the model.

The remainder of this chapter is structured as follows. In the section on the demand side we set out the intertemporal utility maximization problem, from which the consumption function and system of demand equations is derived. Also in this section, we use the indirect utility function to derive a true cost of living index, which is used as a measure of the

---

[1]This comment applies more to the utility function than to the transformation function in its most general form.

aggregate price level. We then set out the producer maximization problem and derive the system of supply equations. The income identity is discussed in the following section, and then the expressions for the trade flows in each commodity and the trade balance are presented. Finally, we give a summary of the model.

The Demand Side[1]

Following Dornbusch and Mussa (1974; hereafter, DM), we assume that the representative consumer chooses the path of consumption and real wealth holdings to maximize the present value of the flow of utility subject to a wealth constraint.[2] The wealth constraint states that the rate of change of wealth equals the difference between income and consumption. The instantaneous utility function has as its arguments consumption and scalar real wealth holdings. Wealth is assumed to be non-interest bearing and yield only non-pecuniary services, and this is the reason for including it directly in the utility function.

Departing from DM, we assume that the household consumes n individually distinguished commodities $x_i (i = 1, \ldots, n)$, and that the instantaneous utility function is of the Klein-Rubin (1947) form:

$$u(x, w) = \sum_{i=1}^{n} \beta_i \ln(x_i - \gamma_i) + \beta_{n+1} \ln(w - \gamma_{n+1})$$

$$\beta_i > 0, \quad (x_i - \gamma_i) > 0 \quad i = 1, \ldots, n,$$

$$\beta_{n+1} > 0, \quad (w - \gamma_{n+1}) > 0,$$

---

[1]This section draws heavily on Dornbusch and Mussa (1975), as it will be apparent.

[2]In fact in DM's model, the only way of holding wealth is in the form of real cash balances. However, the extension to a more general (scalar) wealth concept is immediate.

in which x is an n-vector of the quantities consumed, w is the stock of
real wealth, and the β's and γ's are parameters.[1] This functional form
is used because, firstly, it yields tractible results, and, secondly, it
generates the linear expenditure system which has been widely used in applied demand analysis with much success, and has proven to be a useful
empirical tool.[2]

We assume that the representative consumer holds static expectations with respect to income and all prices, and write the wealth constraint as

$$\frac{dw(t)}{dt} \equiv \dot{w}(t) = y - \tilde{p}'x(t).$$

This states that the rate of change of wealth holdings equals real income,
y, less real consumption, $\tilde{p}'x(t)$, where $\tilde{p} = [p_i/P]$, an n-vector of commodity prices deflated by an appropriate aggregate price index, P.[3] The
question of what is the appropriate aggregate price level is taken up
later.

Formally, the household problem is to choose $x_i(t)$ $(i = 1, \ldots, n)$
and $w(t)$ to

$$\text{Max} \int_o^\infty e^{-\delta t} [\sum_{i=1}^{n+1} \beta_i \ln q_i(t)]dt$$

---

[1]Unless stated otherwise, throughout the dissertation we use Greek
letters to denote parameters and Latin for variables.

[2]See, e.g., Brown and Deaton (1972) for a survey of this empirical
work.

[3]Throughout the dissertation we use the following matrix notation:
vectors are written as columns, a prime denotes transportation, the typical
element of a vector is denoted by a square bracketed variable with one subscript, and the typical element of a matrix is similarly denoted, except
that it has two subscripts.

$$\text{s.t.} \quad \dot{q}_{n+1}(t) = y - \sum_{i=1}^{n} \tilde{p}_i [q_i(t) + \gamma_i]^1$$

$$q_{n+1}(o) = \bar{w} - \gamma_{n+1}, \text{ given.}$$

The following notation has been used in the above:

$$q_i = \begin{cases} x_i - \gamma_i & i = 1, \ldots, n \\ \\ w - \gamma_{n+1} & i = n+1, \quad \text{and} \end{cases}$$

δ is the subjective rate of discount.

The Hamiltonian for this problem is

$$\left[\sum_{i=1}^{n+1} \beta_i \ln q_i + \lambda\{y - \sum_{i=1}^{n} \tilde{p}_i(q_i + \gamma_i)\} \right] e^{-\delta t},$$

where λ is a multiplier. The first order conditions are

$$(2.1) \qquad \frac{\beta_i}{q_i} - \lambda \tilde{p}_i = 0 \quad i = 1, \ldots, n$$

$$(2.2) \qquad \dot{q}_{n+1} = y - \sum_{i=1}^{n} \tilde{p}_i(q_i + \gamma_i)$$

$$(2.3) \qquad \dot{\lambda} = \lambda\delta - \frac{\beta_{n+1}}{q_{n+1}}.$$

Equation (2.1) requires that at each moment of time the marginal utility of commodity i be proportional to its price, where the factor of proportionality is the marginal utility of income. Equation (2.2) is just a restatement of the wealth constraint.

---

[1]Here we have used $\dot{q}_{n+1} = \dot{w}$, which follows from the definition of q_{n+1}. This relationship will be used subsequently.

These first order conditions can be solved for the endogenous variables in two steps. The first is the determination of how much of income is consumed; this quantity can then be used in the second step which is the allocation of the budget to the individual commodities (the classic consumer demand problem). We derive the consumption function as follows. From equations (2.1) and (2.3) we have

$$(2.4.1) \qquad \frac{\dot{\lambda}}{\lambda} = \delta - \frac{\beta_{n+1}}{\beta_i} \frac{\tilde{p}_i q_i}{q_{n+1}} \qquad i = 1, \ldots, n.$$

Were it not for the presence of $\tilde{p}_i$, the second and third terms on the right of (2.4.1) represent the ratio of the marginal utility of wealth to the marginal utility of commodity i, which can be termed the marginal non-pecuniary rate of return on real wealth (cf. DM, p. 417) in terms of commodity i. However, since, from (2.4.1), this quantity has to equal

$$\delta - \dot{\lambda}/\lambda,$$

which is independent of i, we can omit the "in terms of commodity i" part.

It is useful to multiply the denominator and numerator of the third term in equation (2.4.1) by P, the aggregate price index, and rewrite that equation as

$$(2.4.2) \qquad \frac{\dot{\lambda}}{\lambda} = \delta - \frac{\beta_{n+1}}{\beta_i} \frac{p_i q_i}{P q_{n+1}} \qquad i = 1, \ldots, n,$$

in which we have used the definition of the nominal price of commodity i, $p_i = P\tilde{p}_i$. From this expression, the non-pecuniary return on wealth is a function only of the ratio of supernumerary expenditure on good i ($p_i q_i = p_i x_i - p_i \gamma_i$)[1] to supernumerary nominal wealth holdings ($P q_{n+1} = W - P\gamma_{n+1}$, where $W = Pw$).

---

[1]The term "supernumerary" derives from the interpretation of the

15

Setting $\dot{\lambda} = 0$ in equation (2.4.2), we see that in the long run, consumption and wealth holdings must be such that the subjective rate of discount equal the non-pecuniary rate of return on wealth. Using an asterisk (*) to denote a steady state value, the long run ratio of super-numerary expenditure on commodity i to supernumerary wealth holdings is, from (2.4.2),

$$\frac{P_i q_i^*}{P q_{n+1}^*} = \delta \frac{\beta_i}{\beta_{n+1}} = v_i^* \quad i = 1, \ldots, n,$$

for the velocity of expenditure on good i. DM show that for the scalar consumption case, along the optimal path, consumption velocity is constant, i.e.,

$$v(t) = v^* \; \forall t \geq 0.$$

Their proof involves showing that the path of the endogenous variables along which $v(t) = v^*$ satisfies all the optimality conditions and, hence, is the optimal path. The proof holds exactly for our application, and we use the result to derive the consumption function in a similar way to which DM use it. Hence, even out of the steady state, this ratio also equals the long-run velocity, i.e.,

$$\frac{P_i q_i}{P q_{n+1}} = \delta \frac{\beta_i}{\beta_{n+1}} = v_i \quad i = 1, \ldots, n, \quad \text{or}$$

γ's in the Klein-Rubin utility function as being subsistence quantities in the sense that the consumer only enjoys utility when $q_i > 0$, where

$$q_i = \begin{cases} x_i - \gamma_i & i = 1, \ldots, n \\ \\ w - \gamma_{n+1} & i = n+1, \end{cases}$$

as before.

16

(2.5) $$\tilde{p}_i q_i = v_i q_{n+1} \quad i = 1, \ldots, n.$$

Using (2.5) in (2.2) yields

$$\dot{q}_{n+1} = - \sum_{i=1}^{n} v_i q_{n+1} - \sum_{i=1}^{n} \tilde{p}_i \gamma_i + y$$

(2.6) $$= -\alpha q_{n+1} + s,$$

in which

$$\alpha = \frac{\delta}{\beta_{n+1}} \sum_{i=1}^{n} \beta_i, \text{ a constant, and}$$

$$s = y - \sum_{i=1}^{n} \tilde{p}_i \gamma_i.$$

The solution to the differential equation (2.6) is

$$q_{n+1}(t) = q_{n+1}^* + e^{-\alpha t} (\bar{q}_{n+1} - q_{n+1}^*),$$

in which

(2.7.1) $$q_{n+1}^* = s/\alpha, \text{ and}$$

$$\bar{q}_{n+1} = \bar{w} - \gamma_{n+1}, \text{ initial supernumerary wealth holdings.}$$

From (2.7.1) we obtain

$$s = \alpha q_{n+1}^*,$$

and using this in (2.6) gives

(2.7.2) $$\dot{q}_{n+1} = \alpha(q_{n+1}^* - q_{n+1})$$

$$= \alpha(w^* - w),$$

where $w^* = q_{n+1}^* + \gamma_{n+1}$, and where we have used the definition $w = q_{n+1} + \gamma_{n+1}$.

Substituting (2.7.2) in the wealth constraint (2.2) yields the consumption function:

$$(2.8) \qquad c = y + \alpha(w - w^*),$$

in which $c = \sum_{i=1}^{n} \tilde{p}_i x_i$, real consumption.

Equation (2.8) states that consumption equals income plus a constant fraction α of the gap between actual and long-run desired wealth.[1] In the long-run, when desired and actual wealth are equal (stock equilibrium), income is totally consumed—the long-run average propensity to consume is unity. Hence, if, for example, the actual stock of wealth is greater than that desired in the long run, the household gets rid of the excess wealth over time by consuming more than its income. The actual stock approaches the desired stock at an exponential rate. The reason why w does not jump to its desired level instantaneously is twofold. First, it may not be feasible if the desired increment in wealth is greater than income.[2] Second, it is always optimal to smooth the consumption path, due to diminishing marginal utility of consumption, and this rules out jumps in the wealth stock caused by foregoing consumption.[3]

The consumption function (2.8) is essentially the same as DM's equation (22). We do, however, have some more information on our coefficient α--we know what it is in terms of utility function parameters, since an

---

[1] This type of consumption function, only with wealth replaced by real cash balances, has been used by Prais (1961) and Mundell (1968, Chap. VIII), among others, in analyzing the real balance effect. The general notion of the wealth-saving relationship comes from Metzler (1951).

[2] Here we are speaking loosely because instantaneously the stock of wealth is fixed, and it can only be changed over time by saving, which is a flow.

[3] The comments in the previous footnote also apply here.

explicit functional form is used. In particular, α is the product of the subjective rate of discount (δ) and the ratio of the sum of the β's for the commodities ($\sum_{i=1}^{n} \beta_i$) to the elasticity of instantaneous utility with respect to supernumerary real wealth holdings, $w - \gamma_{n+1}$; this elasticity is β_{n+1}. The parameter α has the interpretation of being the speed of adjustment of wealth holdings and consumption to their long-run values. Hence, the higher is the subjective discount rate and the marginal utility of consumption, and the lower is the marginal utility of wealth,[1] the faster will a gap between w and w^* be closed. These results are quite specific to the model and follow from the relationship of α to the consumption-wealth ratio.[2]

The expression for the long-run desired wealth is given by equation (2.7.1), which can be rewritten as

$$(2.9) \qquad w^* = \gamma_{n+1} + \frac{1}{\alpha}\left(y - \sum_{i=1}^{n} \bar{p}_i \gamma_i\right).$$

Hence, desired wealth is a linear function of income and all prices in the system.

The saving function, or the flow demand for wealth, is given by equation (2.7.2) which can be rewritten as

$$(2.10) \qquad \dot{w} = \alpha(w^* - w)$$

$$(2.11) \qquad = y - \sum_{i=1}^{n} \bar{p}_i \gamma_i - \alpha(w - \gamma_{n+1}),$$

---

[1] The instantaneous marginal utility of good i is a monotonically increasing function of β_i. Similarly, the instantaneous marginal utility of real wealth holdings is monotonically increasing in β_{n+1}.

[2] That is,

$$\alpha = \left(c - \sum_{i=1}^{n} \bar{p}_i \gamma_i\right)/(w - \gamma_{n+1}).$$

from (2.9). Notice that the saving function (2.10) is just the complement of the consumption function (2.8) in the sense that the part of income not consumed is saved. This is exactly as it should be.

It can be seen from the saving function in the form of equation (2.11) that any increment to income is saved in the short run, i.e., $\partial \dot{w}/\partial y = 1$. The reason for this is that supernumerary expenditure is always proportional to supernumerary wealth holdings [see equation (2.5)], and any increment to income has to be saved in the short run; it is only after a finite amount of time that the stock of wealth increases, and it is only then that consumption can increase, hence maintaining the proportionality relationship. This result means that, in this model, wealth acts as a buffer stock for consumption.

We now turn to the derivation of the demand equations for individual commodities. To do this, we solve the n first order conditions contained in system (2.1) and use the requirement that total consumption must equal c, as determined by equation (2.8), the consumption function. Using the definition $q_i = x_i - \gamma_i$ $(i = 1, \ldots, n)$, (2.1) can be rearranged to give

$$(2.12) \qquad \tilde{p}_i x_i = \lambda^{-1} \beta_i + \tilde{p}_i \gamma_i \qquad i = 1, \ldots, n.$$

Adding both sides of system (2.12) over all commodities, substituting c for $\Sigma \tilde{p}_i x_i$, and rearranging yields

$$\lambda^{-1} = (c - \sum_{i=1}^{n} \tilde{p}_i \gamma_i)/(\sum_{i=1}^{n} \beta_i).$$

Substituting this expression for λ^{-1} back into (2.12) gives one version of the system of expenditure equations:

$$(2.13) \qquad \tilde{p}_i x_i = \tilde{p}_i \gamma_i + \theta_i (c - \sum_{j=1}^{n} \tilde{p}_j \gamma_j) \qquad i = 1, \ldots, n,$$

in which
$$\theta_i = \beta_i / (\sum_{j=1}^{n} \beta_j).$$

Multiplying both sides of (2.13) by P, the aggregate price index, converts the deflated prices to money prices and real total consumption to a nominal magnitude:

$$(2.14) \qquad v_i = p_i \gamma_i + \theta_i (C - \sum_{j=1}^{n} p_j \gamma_j) \quad i = 1, \ldots, n,$$

in which

$$v_i = p_i x_i, \text{ expenditure on commodity i, and}$$
$$C = Pc = \sum_{i=1}^{n} v_i, \text{ total consumption expenditure.}$$

System (2.14) is Stone's (1954) linear expenditure system (LES), and it states that expenditure on each commodity is a linear function of all prices and total expenditure. Some of the properties of LES are as follows [Powell (1974b)]. The θ's are the marginal budget shares and, hence, sum to unity. Under the utility function specification, each θ has to be positive, ruling out inferior goods. All commodities in LES are gross complements and net substitutes--income effects outweight substitution effects. If all the γ's are positive, each uncompensated own-price demand elasticity is less than unity in absolute value. Although these properties are somewhat restrictive (and are related to the direct additivity of the Klein-Rubin utility function), LES should be satisfactory if applied to broad commodity groups, since these properties become more plausible the higher is the level of aggregation (i.e., the smaller is the number of individually distinguished commodities).

Since LES is derived from a utility function, it automatically

satisfies the budget constraint, homogeneity and symmetry. In fact, LES
is the only expenditure system which is linear in prices and total expenditure which satisfies globally these demand theory restrictions
[Goldberger (1967)]. Therefore, LES has the advantage of simplicity.

Finally, the total expenditure elasticities in LES are potentially
non-unitary. This is because the Klein-Rubin is not homothetic to the
origin, but to the γ's. This utility function property is termed "marginal
homotheticity." As was mentioned previously, the γ-parameters are sometimes given the physical interpretation of being subsistence consumption in
the sense that the utility function is defined only when $x_i > \gamma_i$ ($i = 1$,
. . . , n).[1] This interpretation, however, breaks down when the γ's are
negative.

For subsequent use, let us rewrite the consumption function, equation (2.8), and the expression for long-run desired wealth, equation (2.9),
in nominal terms as

(2.15) $$C = Y + \alpha(W - W^*),$$

in which

C = cP, total consumption expenditure,

Y = yP, nominal income,

W = wP, nominal wealth, and

W^* = w^*P, long-run desired nominal wealth;

(2.16) $$W^* = P\gamma_{n+1} + \frac{1}{\alpha} \left(Y - \sum_{i=1}^{n} P_i\gamma_i \right).$$

---

[1]The term "subsistence" really requires quotation marks since,
in cross-country studies, estimates of the cost of subsistence (in the
LES sense) have been found to be positively related to income. See Lluch,
Powell, and Williams (1977, Chap. IV).

Also for subsequent use, let us write this consumption function solely in terms of observable variables by substituting (2.16) into (2.15) to give

$$(2.17) \qquad C = \sum_{i=1}^{n} p_i \gamma_i + \alpha(W - P\gamma_{n+1}).$$

From this it can be seen that total expenditure is a function of the individual commodity prices. It can also be seen that, in the short run, consumption is unaffected by income, as was previously discussed.

We now take up the question of the choice of an appropriate aggregate price index P. Since we are working with an explicit functional form for the utility function, a natural choice for this index is the utility constant or true cost of living index. To simplify the problem, we use a conditional index, which comes from the theory of subindexes of the cost of living [Pollak (1975)]. This index has all the properties of a traditional cost of living index, and it is defined as the ratio of expenditure on current goods required to attain a given level of utility in the light of price changes, when the consumption of future goods is held constant. However, in our case, with intertemporal separability of the utility function, it can be shown that the conditional index has the additional property of being independent of future consumption [Pollak (1975)].

This means that we can use the initial $(t = 0)$ Klein-Rubin utility function to obtain an expression for total expenditure as a function of the utility level and prices. We then use this expression to obtain the required expenditure to keep utility constant when prices change, and the ratio of the two levels of expenditure is the conditional index. There is, however, a problem in directly implementing this procedure. Total expenditure is a function of the individual commodity prices via their effect on W^* [see equation (2.17)]. This means that we need to substitute the consumption function into the demand equations to obtain the total or "reduced form" effects of prices. When we do this, however, both total expenditure and income drop out from the system [income does not appear on the consumption function as written in equation (2.17)]. As a result, the only variables effecting demand in this reduced form sense are prices and wealth, so that it is not possible to invert the indirect utility function and solve for expenditure in terms of utility and prices. The procedure we adopt is to solve the indirect utility function for wealth and use the ratio of the two levels of wealth as the conditional index. This appears to be the natural solution when total expenditure is endogenous; we can take the stock of wealth as predetermined since it is fixed instantaneously.

The "reduced form" expenditure equations[1] are obtained by substituting the consumption function in its equation (2.17) form into LES, system (2.14). This gives

$$(2.18) \qquad v_i = p_i \gamma_i + \alpha \theta_i (W - P\gamma_{n+1}) \qquad i = 1, \ldots, n.$$

The initial instantaneous utility function is

$$(2.19) \qquad u = \sum_{i=1}^{n} \beta_i \ln(x_i - \gamma_i) + \beta_{n+1} \ln(w - \gamma_{n+1}).$$

To be able to obtain our results, we need to assume that wealth is denominated in real terms, so that w is invariant to changes in the aggregate price level.[2] With the exception of assets like outside money, this

---

[1]These are only partial reduced forms in the econometric sense, because, from the viewpoint of the complete model, some prices are endogenous. However, for the development of the demand side of the model, consumers are assumed to take all prices as exogenous.

[2]Note that this is compatible with the earlier assumption of a zero real rate of return on wealth.

specification is probably quite reasonable in the aggregate. The reason is that, in general equilibrium, most capital gains and losses on assets denominated in nominal terms due to changes in the price level net out to zero. Under this assumption, (2.19) can be written as

$$(2.20) \qquad u = \Sigma \beta_i \ln(x_i - \gamma_i) + k,$$

in which

$$k = \beta_{n+1} \ln(w - \gamma_{n+1}), \text{ a constant.}[1]$$

Substituting the demand equations associated with system (2.18) into (2.20) yields the indirect utility function, which is

$$u = \sum_{j=1}^{n} \beta_j [k_1 + \ln(W - P\gamma_{n+1}) - \sum_{i=1}^{n} \theta_i \ln p_i],$$

in which k_1 is another constant. Solving this for W as a function of u and p_i gives

$$W = P\gamma_{n+1} + k_2 \prod_{i=1}^{n} p_i^{\theta_i}$$

in which

$$k_2 = \exp[u(\Sigma \beta_i)^{-1} - k_1], \text{ a constant.}$$

Denoting two sets of prices and the associated wealth required to keep utility constant by a zero and one subscript, in this situation the conditional index is

$$(2.21) \qquad W_1/W_0 = \frac{P_1 \gamma_{n+1} + k_2 \Pi p_{i1}^{\theta_i}}{P_0 \gamma_{n+1} + k_2 \Pi p_{i0}^{\theta_i}}.$$

---

[1] An alternative reason for treating w as a constant here is that instantaneously it is fixed, as mentioned before.

Now, if we choose to use the conditional index for the aggregate price index, we have

$$P_1/P_0 = W_1/W_0,$$

or, using (2.21) and setting all initial prices equal to unity for convenience,

$$P_1(1 - \frac{\gamma_{n+1}}{\gamma_{n+1} + k_2}) = \frac{k_2}{\gamma_{n+1} + k_2} \prod p_i^{\theta_i},$$

or

(2.22)
$$P_1 = \prod_{i=1}^{n} P_{i1}^{\theta_i}.$$

Hence, the conditional index simplifies to a Divisia index of the individual commodity prices, with the marginal budget shares as weights.

The Supply Side

In this section, we first characterize the technology of the economy by assuming a particular functional form for the transformation function. The transformation function is then used to solve for the competitive equilibrium production point by deriving the general equilibrium supply equations.

The reason why we represent technology by writing down a transformation function directly, rather than deriving it by solving the factor market equilibrium conditions, as is usual in international trade theory, is that it is not possible to represent the transformation function in closed form by solving these equilibrium conditions. It is assumed that the transformation function is a quadratic form in the output of each of the n sectors:[1]

---

[1]Johnson (1965) uses a variant of this functional form in a two sector model application.

(2.23) $$z' \Lambda z = K^2 \qquad \Lambda = \Lambda',$$

in which

> $z = [z_i]$, an n-vector of outputs,
>
> Λ is a positive definite symmetric matrix of
> parameters, and
>
> K is a positive scalar.

There is no loss of generality in specifying that Λ is symmetric because if it were not symmetric, the form takes the same value if Λ is replaced by the symmetric matrix $\frac{1}{2}(\Lambda + \Lambda')$ [see, e.g., Theil (1971, p. 21)].

The term K in (2.23) determines the distance of the transformation surface from the origin, and it represents the aggregate resource endowment of the economy. It should be noted also that K is a neutral shifter of the transformation surface in the sense that variations in K leave undisturbed all marginal rates of transformation along a given ray from the origin. As a result, if relative prices are constant, growth of the economy, as represented by increases in K, does not change the relative production pattern—all output elasticities with respect to K are unity.[1]

In the n = 2 commodities case, equation (2.23) defines a circle if Λ is a scalar matrix (i.e., $\Lambda = \lambda I$), and an ellipse if Λ is a general diagonal matrix (i.e., $\Lambda = \text{diag}[\lambda_1 \ \lambda_2]'$).

The final point to note about equation (2.23) is that Diewert (1974) has extensively analyzed this functional form, and he shows that it is a

---

[1]A possible extension of this framework to allow for many factor inputs and to make the input demands endogenous is to write K as a function of these inputs. This function would be something similar to a conventional one output production function, defining the quantity of generalized output, K. This could then be used in conjunction with equation (2.23). An approach along these lines is taken by Dixon, Vincent and Powell (1976).

flexible functional form in the sense that it provides a second order local approximation to an arbitrary transformation function, given some weak regularity conditions.

We view producers as choosing the composition of output to maximize its value subject to the transformation function and parametric prices. One interpretation of this setup is as follows: there are many competitive firms in the economy and their production behavior can be modeled as if they all produce some of each commodity, and the transformation function is a multiple output production function of the representative firm.

Formally, this maximization problem is

$$\text{Max } p'z$$
$$z$$
$$\text{s.t. } z' \Lambda z = K^2,$$

in which $p = [p_i]$, an n-vector of prices. Define the Lagrangean

$$L = p'z - \mu(z'\Lambda z - K^2),$$

in which μ is a (scalar) Lagrange multiplier. The first order conditions for a maximum are

(2.24) $p = 2\mu \Lambda z$

(2.25) $z'\Lambda z = K^2.$

Equation (2.24) states that z is to be chosen to set marginal cost equal to price, while (2.25) is just a restatement of the transformation function.

Rearranging (2.24) yields

(2.26) $z = (2\mu)^{-1}\Lambda^{-1} p,$

and substituting this into (2.25) gives

$$(2.27) \qquad (2\mu)^{-2} \, p'\Lambda^{-1}\Lambda\Lambda^{-1} \, p = K^2,$$

where we have used the fact that Λ is symmetric. Solving (2.27) for μ^{-1} yields

$$\mu^{-1} = \frac{2K}{(p'\Lambda^{-1} p)^{1/2}},$$

and substituting this back into (2.26) gives the system of supply equations

$$(2.28) \qquad z = \frac{K}{(p'\Phi p)^{1/2}} \, \Phi \, p,$$

in which $\Phi = \Lambda^{-1}$, a positive definite symmetric matrix of parameters.

It can be shown that this supply system is homogenous of degree zero in nominal prices, as it should be. A further property is that the cross slopes are symmetric, which is analogous to the result of consumer demand theory of symmetry of the substitution effects.

The Income Identity

The demand and production parts of the model are linked by the income identity. This identity is also the vehicle by which money enters the model. This is because it is assumed that increases in the stock of domestic credit get into the system _via_ direct transfers and, hence, raise income directly. This helicopter-drop-type assumption can be justified in at least two ways. Increases in domestic credit will constitute an increment to income if these changes are brought about by open market operations involving government bonds, and if these do not represent net wealth to the economy as a whole, due to their associated future taxes. Another justification, which is independent of the discounting of future taxes, is if domestic credit is expanded by the Treasury borrowing from the monetary authority and then spending the proceeds; i.e., if domestic credit is increased via government spending. Including changes in domestic credit as a component of disposable income is the open economy analogue of the Sidrauski (1967) definition of income.[1]

As previously discussed, wealth is taken to be denominated in real terms so that its real value is invariant to changes in the price level. Hence, we also include in the definition of nominal income changes in the nominal value of wealth due to inflation, $\hat{P}W$, where $\hat{P}$ is the percentage change in P, the aggregate price index. It should be noted that including $\hat{P}W$ in income is really only an accounting convention; an alternative procedure would be to include this term directly in the wealth accumulation relationship, when expressed in nominal terms. The latter procedure, however, is in every way equivalent to including the term in income. The reason is that an implication of the model is that $\hat{P}W$, if included in income, will be totally saved (recall that the impact MPC is zero), and hence indirectly go into the wealth accumulation relationship. This is exactly as it should be since $\hat{P}W$ is not income available for consumption—it has to be totally saved in order to restore the real value of wealth.

Nominal income is therefore the sum of the value of output, the rate of change in the domestic credit component of the monetary base, and $\hat{P}W$:

$$(2.29) \qquad Y = \sum_{i=1}^{n} p_i z_i + \dot{D} + \hat{P}W,$$

---

[1]Sjaastad (1975), in a more extended model along these lines, draws a distinction between whether the government does or does not capture all the proceeds of the additional credit. Our model allows no scope for this distinction because we do not have an explicit government sector.

in which $\overset{.}{D}$ is the rate of change in the domestic credit component of the
monetary base. The reason for excluding from income the other component
of the monetary base, foreign assets, is that this variable is endogenous,
not under the control of the domestic monetary authority.

The Trade Flows and the Trade Balance

Those goods which have a positive domestic excess supply at the
parametric world prices are exported, those whose domestic excess supply
is negative are imported, and the commodities which have a zero domestic
excess supply are nontraded goods. Denoting by ψ the subset of commodities which are traded, the value of the trade flows can be written as

$$(2.30) \qquad p_i z_i - v_i = \begin{cases} e_i & i \in \psi \\ 0 & i \notin \psi \end{cases}$$

where e_i is the value of exports ($e_i > 0$) or imports ($e_i < 0$) of commodity i. Setting the nontraded goods domestic excess supplies to zero
means that their prices, $p_i (i \notin \psi)$, are endogenous variables of the model.

The final identity of the model is for the trade balance. This
states that the trade balance is the value of exports less the value of
imports:

$$(2.31) \qquad B = \sum_{i \in \psi} e_i .$$

We will now show that the model is consistent in the sense that the
trade balance equals the difference between the value of output and expenditure. This means that the economy's budget constraint is satisfied.
Substituting equations (2.30), (2.29), and (2.14) into (2.31), and using
the market clearing requirement for the nontraded goods given in (2.30),
yields

$$(2.32) \qquad B = Y - \dot{D} - \hat{P}W - C.$$

This states that the trade balance is the difference between the value of output $(Y - \dot{D} - \hat{P}W)$ and expenditure.

Summary

To summarize, the model is made up of a consumption function, an expression for the long-run desired stock of wealth, a wealth accumulation relationship, n domestic expenditure equations, one for each commodity, an expression for the aggregate price level, n domestic supply equations, an income identity, an expression for the value of the trade flow for each of the internationally trade commodities, and, finally, a domestic market clearing condition for each of the nontraded goods.

For the convenience of having it all in one place, in Table 1 we give the entire model. Here, everything is expressed in nominal terms. All these equations have appeared in this form previously except for the rate of change of wealth expression. This can be written in nominal terms in the form given in the table since we have included in income the increase in the nominal value of wealth due to inflation, $\hat{P}W$.[1]

The model is a system of $(6 + 3n)$ simultaneous equations. We give the $(6 + 3n)$ endogenous variables in Table 2; all the remaining variables are predetermined and are given in Table 3.

---

[1]The expression given in the table is obtained straightforwardly as follows. From the definition of real wealth $w = W/P$,

$$\dot{w} = w(\hat{W} - \hat{P}),$$

in which a "^" denotes a percentage rate of change, as before. Combining this with the wealth constraint written in real terms, equation (2.2), and using the definition of income, equation (2.29), yields the expression in the table.

TABLE 1

THE MODEL[a]

Consumption

$$C = Y + \alpha(W - W^*)$$

Long-run Desired Wealth

$$W^* = P\gamma_{n+1} + \frac{1}{\alpha} (Y - \sum_{i=1}^{n} p_i\gamma_i)$$

Rate of Change of Wealth

$$\dot{W} = Y - C$$

Expenditure System

$$v_i = p_i\gamma_i + \theta_i(C - \sum_{j=1}^{n} p_j\gamma_j) \quad i = 1, \ldots, n$$

$$\sum_{i=1}^{n} \theta_i = 1$$

Aggregate Price Index

$$P = \prod_{i=1}^{n} p_i^{\theta_i}$$

Supply System

$$z_i = \frac{K}{(p'\Phi p)^{1/2}} \sum_{j=1}^{n} \phi_{ij}p_j \quad i = 1, \ldots, n$$

$$\Phi = \Phi', \quad x'\Phi x > 0 \text{ for any } x \neq 0$$

$$\text{in which } \Phi = [\phi_{ij}]$$

Income

$$Y = \sum_{i=1}^{n} p_i z_i + \dot{D} + \hat{P}W$$

Trade Flows

$$p_i z_i - v_i = \begin{cases} e_i & i\varepsilon\psi \\ 0 & i\cancel{\varepsilon}\psi \end{cases}$$

Trade Balance

$$B = \sum_{i\varepsilon\psi} e_i$$

---

[a]See Tables 2 and 3 for meaning of notation.

TABLE 2

THE ENDOGENOUS VARIABLES

Variable	Description
C	Consumption
W^*	Long-run desired wealth
$\dot{W}$	Rate of change of wealth
v_i (i = 1, . . . , n)	Domestic expenditure on commodity i
P	Aggregate price index
z_i (i = 1, . . . , n)	Output of sector i
Y	Income
e_i (i$\epsilon\psi$)	Value of trade flow in good i
p_i (i$\ell\psi$)	Price of nontraded good i
B	Trade balance

TABLE 3

THE PREDETERMINED VARIABLES

Variable	Description
W	Wealth
K	Aggregate resource endowment
$\dot{D}$	Rate of change in domestic credit component of monetary base
p_i (i$\epsilon\psi$)	Price of traded good i

CHAPTER III

ECONOMETRIC RESULTS

Introduction

In this chapter we make the theoretical model of the previous chapter operational, i.e., capable of being estimated with actual data, by introducing some real world complexities which we previously ignored. We then estimate the parameters of the model with U.S. annual data for the post-war period. Finally, the fitted model is simulated over the sample period to determine its tracking ability.

The chapter is structured as follows. First, the modifications required to make the model operational are set out. Second, stochastic specification and estimation procedures are discussed. Third, we give some details of the data base which we use in estimation. Fourth, empirical results are given, and finally we give some concluding comments.

Empirical Implementation

In the previous chapter we abstracted from investment in real capital, and government expenditure and taxation. We take account of these in the simplest possible way. Investment is taken as exogenous, but we continue to abstract from the consequences of this investment on the stock of capital. The government sector is consolidated in with the rest of the economy. That is, we divide up government expenditure into a consumption part and an investment part, and then add those to the corresponding private expenditures; all taxation drops out when we consolidate.

34

Denoting by v_i^i expenditure on the output of sector i for investment purposes, by v_i^c consumption expenditure on the ith commodity, and by v_i total expenditure, we now have

(3.1)
$$v_i = v_i^i + v_i^c \qquad i = 1, \ldots, n.$$

The only notational change required to be made in the previous chapter now is to replace v_i in LES, system (2.14), with v_i^c.

With investment in the model, the consumption function (2.15) is no longer an appropriate representation since it states that in full equilibrium consumption equals income. A more reasonable long-run property is that total expenditure (consumption plus investment) equal income; we incorporate this property by replacing C in equation (2.15) with total expenditure, to be denoted by A, for absorption, which is defined as

$$A = C + I,$$

where $I = \sum_{i=1}^{n} v_i^i$, total investment expenditure which is taken as exogenous.[1]

A further modification required to make the model operational is to include interest income on net holdings of foreign securities (the surplus on the debt service account) in the definition of income, equation (2.29). We denote this variable by DS and take it as exogenous.

We eliminate the unobservable variable in the model, W^*, long-run desired wealth, by substituting it out from the system.

The model is a system of simultaneous equations which is nonlinear in the parameters, endogenous and predetermined variables. In addition, there are restrictions on the parameters both within and across equations.

---

[1]C is still the (endogenous) variable which appears in LES, system (2.14).

To simplify the computational problems of estimating such a model, we linearize in terms of variables; i.e., we expand each equation as a Taylor series around a convenient coordinate set and drop higher order terms. The coordinate set which we use is sample means. We retain, however, all restrictions on the parameters in the linearized model.

The operational model, incorporating the above modifications, is given in Table 4. Here, sample means are denoted by a bar and units are chosen such that all prices have unit means. All constant terms which result from the linearization are denoted by κ_i. In the table, all time derivatives have been replaced with finite first differences, denoted by $\Delta x = x - x_{-1}$ for any variable x. Finally, we have replaced W in the definition of income with its lagged value; this is done for the pragmatic reason that it simplifies the construction of the income series.

The linearized model is a system of (6 + 4n) simultaneous equations. We give the (6 + 4n) endogenous variables in Table 5, and the predetermined variable in Table 6.

Stochastic Specification and Estimation Procedures

The operational model, although linear in the variables, is nonlinear in the parameters. In addition, there are within and across equations restrictions on the parameters. These characteristics mean that the most convenient estimator to use is full information maximum likelihood (FIML).

After adding disturbance terms, it is convenient to write the model (after eliminating identities) as[1]

---

[1]All notation in this section is new, unrelated to that used previously.

TABLE 4

THE OPERATIONAL MODEL[a]

Absorption

$$A = \sum_{i=1}^{n} p_i \gamma_i + \alpha(W - P\gamma_{n+1})$$

Consumption

$$C = A - I$$

Wealth

$$W = W_{-1} + Y - C$$

Expenditure System

$$v_i^c = p_i \gamma_i + \theta_i (C - \sum_{j=1}^{n} p_j \gamma_j) \quad i = 1, \ldots, n$$

$$\sum_{i=1}^{n} \theta_i = 1$$

Aggregate Price Index

$$P = \kappa_1 + \sum_{i=1}^{n} \theta_i p_i$$

Supply System

$$z_i = \kappa_{i+1} + [\bar{z}_i(\phi_{ii}/\phi_{i.} - \phi_{i.}/\phi_{..})]p_i + \sum_{j \neq i} [\bar{z}_i(\phi_{ij}/\phi_{i.} - \phi_{j.}/\phi_{..})]p_j$$

$$+ (\bar{z}_i/\bar{K})K \quad i = 1, \ldots, n$$

$$\phi = \phi', \quad x'\phi x > 0 \quad \text{for any} \quad x \neq 0,$$

in which

$$\phi_{i.} = \sum_{j=1}^{n} \phi_{ij},$$

$$\phi_{..} = \sum_{i=1}^{n} \phi_{i.},$$

TABLE 4.--Continued

and

$$\Phi = [\phi_{ij}]$$

Income

$$Y = \kappa_{n+2} + \sum_{i=1}^{n} (z_i + \bar{z}_i p_i) + \Delta D + DS + \bar{W}_{-1}(\Delta P) + (\Delta \bar{P})W_{-1}$$

Total Expenditures

$$v_i = v_i^i + v_i^c \qquad i = 1, \ldots, n$$

Trade Flows

$$\kappa_{i+n+2} + z_i + \bar{z}_i p_i - v_i = \begin{cases} e_i & i\epsilon\psi \\ \\ 0 & i\not\epsilon\psi \end{cases}$$

Trade Balance

$$B = \sum_{i\epsilon\psi} e_i$$

[a]See Tables 5 and 6 for meaning of notation.

TABLE 5

ENDOGENOUS VARIABLES OF OPERATIONAL MODEL

Variable	Description
A	Absorption
C	Consumption
W	Wealth
v_i^c (i = 1, . . . , n)	Domestic consumption expenditure on commodity i
P	Aggregate price index
z_i (i = 1, . . . , n)	Output of sector i
Y	Income
v_i (i = 1, . . . , n)	Total domestic expenditure on commodity i
e_i (iεψ)	Value of trade flow in good i
p_i (i∉ψ)	Price of nontraded good i
B	Trade balance

TABLE 6

PREDETERMINED VARIABLES OF OPERATIONAL MODEL

Variable	Description
I	Total domestic investment expenditure
W_{-1}	Lagged wealth
K	Aggregate resource endowment
ΔD	Change in domestic credit component of monetary base
DS	Debt Service surplus
v_i^i (i = 1, . . . , n)	Domestic investment expenditure on commodity i
p_i (iεψ)	Price of traded good i

(3.2) $\qquad A(\theta)y_t + B(\theta)z_t = u_t \qquad t = 0, \ldots, T,$

in which, at time t, y_t is a vector of endogenous variables, z_t a vector
of predetermined variables, u_t a vector of zero mean stochastic disturbance
terms, and $A(\theta)$ and $B(\theta)$ are comformable coefficient matrices, the elements
of which are (nonlinear) functions of the parameter vector θ.

The u's are assumed to follow a first order vector autoregressive
process:

(3.3) $\qquad\qquad\qquad u_t = \rho u_{t-1} + v_t,$

in which ρ is a parameter matrix, and v_t is an error vector with the
following properties:

$\qquad E(v_t) = 0,$

$\qquad E(v_t v'_{t'}) = \delta_{tt'}\Omega,$ where $\delta_{tt'}$ is the Kronecker delta, and Ω is a

$\qquad\qquad\qquad\qquad$ general positive definite covariance matrix, and

$\qquad v_t \sim N(0, \Omega),$

for t, t' = 1, $\ldots$, T. In words, the v's are zero mean, contemporaneously correlated, serially uncorrelated, have a constant covariance
matrix, and are drawn from a multivariate normal distribution.

The model can be transformed so that its disturbance are white
noise as follows. Lagging system (3.2) one period, multiplying it by ρ,
subtracting the result from (3.2), and then using (3.3) yields

(3.4) $\quad A(\theta)y_t - \rho A(\theta)y_{t-1} + B(\theta)z_t - \rho B(\theta)z_{t-1} = v_t \qquad t = 1, \ldots , T.$

The disturbances in this transformed system are classical; it can be seen
that the autoregressive transformation introduces a further nonlinearity
in the parameters.

Taking the first observation on the endogenous variables as fixed, the log-likelihood function associated with system (3.4) is

$$(3.5) \quad L(Y|\theta, \rho, \Omega) = \text{constant} - \frac{T}{2} \ln|\Omega| + T \ln|A|$$

$$- \frac{1}{2} \sum_{t=1}^{T} (Ay_t - \rho Ay_{t-1} + Bz_t - \rho Bz_{t-1})' \Omega^{-1} (Ay_t - \rho Ay_{t-1} + Bz_t - \rho Bz_{t-1}),$$

in which $Y = [y_1 \ldots y_T]$, a matrix of observations on all the endogenous variables. The full information maximum likelihood estimates of θ, ρ and Ω are those which maximize (3.5). This maximization is a nonlinear problem requiring numerical methods; we use a Newton-Raphson search procedure to locate the maximum of the likelihood function. The estimation program we use is RESIMUL, written by Wymer (1973).

We employ two reparameterizations in estimation. First, positive definitivity of the Φ matrix is enforced by writing it as

$$\Phi = \Pi\Pi',$$

where Π is a lower triangular matrix. The elements of Π, π_{ij}, are then estimated directly. When written in this way, Φ is by definition positive semidefinite.[1] It should be noted that this reparameterization preserves the symmetry of Φ--$\Pi\Pi'$ and Φ both contain $\frac{1}{2} n(n+1)$ distinct elements.

Since the linearized supply equations are homogeneous of degree zero in the parameters ϕ_{ij}, it is not possible to identify them without a normalization. The normalization rule which we use is

$$\sum_i \sum_j \phi_{ij} = 1.$$

---

[1]Barten and Geyskens (1975) discuss the use of this reparameterization in the context of another problem, but they do not empirically implement it.

This means that the π_{ij}'s must satisfy

$$\iota'\Pi\Pi'\iota = 1,$$

in which ι is an n-vector of unit elements. We enforce this constraint by writing one arbitrarily selected π_{ij} in terms of the others.

The second reparameterization relates to the utility function wealth parameter, γ_{n+1}. Since it turns out that the estimate of this parameter is very much larger than the others, to avoid numerical problems associated with large differences in parameter order of magnitudes, we write this as

$$\gamma_{n+1} = \eta_1 \sin^2(\eta_2).$$

We then set η_1 to an arbitrarily large positive value, and estimate η_2 as a parameter. This procedure constrains the γ_{n+1}-estimate to the interval $[0, \eta_1]$. This has the advantage that, although the estimate of γ_{n+1} is large, the η_2-estimate need not be.

The Data Base

To estimate the model, we use U.S. annual data for the period 1952 to 1971.[1] We partition the whole production side of the economy into n=3 sectors which produce exportables, importables and nontraded goods. The output of the exportables sector is either exported or consumed domestically; similarly, domestic demand for importables is satisfied either by the output of the domestic importables sector or by imports.

A good deal of effort was devoted to constructing a data base which is both internally consistent, and consistent with the requirements of the

[1] That is, for the initial observation on the lagged endogenous variables, we use their 1951 value.

theoretical model. Full details of the data are given in the appendix,
and we give only a brief overview here.

The primary source for most of the data is the National Accounts.
We use implicit price deflators for each commodity price index. The
aggregate price index P is constructed as follows. First, we use the GNP
deflator for P to estimate the model. We then use the resulting θ—estimates
together with the three commodity price indexes to form P accoring to
equation (2.22), the Divisia expression.[1]

The output of each sector is constructed by allocating the components of GNP (consumption, investment, government expenditure, exports
and imports) into exportables, importables, nontraded goods, and debt
service. We do this using the highest level of disaggregation available
in the National Accounts: for consumption, for example, we apply the
allocation procedure to the 81 commodity-level data.

The government sector is consolidated in with the private sector by
adding government expenditure to private consumption and investment. We
obtain the consumer demands by reclassifying the disaggregated consumption
data into expenditure on our three commodities. Similarly, for the investment demands.

The wealth variable is constructed recursively by adding gross
savings to the previous period's wealth. We compute an initial value for
wealth by capitalizing permanent income in 1938. Income is defined as GNP
plus the sum of the change in the domestic credit component of high-powered
money and the increase in the nominal value of wealth due to inflation.

---

[1]An alternative procedure would be to substitute out P from the
system. However, θ—values are still required to compute the change in
the nominal value of wealth due to inflation, which, in turn, is needed
to form the income variable [see equation (2.29), the definition of in-
come].

Finally, the number of full-time equivalent employees in all industries is our aggregate factor endowment index.

Some key characteristics of the data base are given in Table 7.
Here, exportables, importables, and nontraded goods are denoted by the
subscript 1, 2, and 3, respectively (we also use this subscripting convention below). All variables (except prices) are deflated by population and
the units of all values are current dollars per capita.

Several comments can be made about the data base, as described in
Table 7. First, it can be seen that, in this three sector setup, nontraded
goods dominate. For both investment and consumption, nontraded goods
represent over one-half of the respective totals. Another notable feature
is that the highest percentage price increase over the sample period is for
nontraded goods also. The mean annual per capita income is about $3,800,
which is approximately 18 percent of mean per capita wealth. At sample
means, there are about three people for every full-time equivalent em-
ployee. Finally, the trade balance is quite volatile over the sample period;
its mean is about $4 per capita.

Empirical Results

For estimation, we use per capita data. The model, as set out in
Table 4, can be written in per capita terms provided we make one minor
modification to the wealth identity to take account of population growth.
Using an asterisk (*) to denote a variable deflated by population, the
wealth identity can be written as

$$W_t^* = \frac{1}{1 + r_t} W_{t-1}^* + Y_t^* - C_t^*,$$

where r_t is the rate of population growth. As an approximation, we assume

TABLE 7

CHARACTERISTICS OF THE DATA BASE[a]

	Absorption and Investment					Consumption				Prices			
	A	v_1^1	v_2^1	v_3^1	I	v_1^c	v_2^c	v_3^c	C	P_1	P_2	P_3	P
1952	2186.47	124.11	24.63	251.54	400.28	250.14	571.80	964.25	1786.19	0.9505	0.9934	0.6992	0.7913
1961	2799.10	146.57	20.29	320.36	487.22	289.65	679.59	1342.64	2311.88	0.9804	0.9598	0.9789	0.9735
1971	5070.67	304.19	38.94	540.92	884.05	428.90	1207.91	2549.81	4186.62	1.2102	1.1938	1.3893	1.3165
Sample Mean	3206.79	196.42	31.95	356.81	585.18	310.45	785.55	1525.61	2621.61	1.0000	1.0000	1.0000	0.9976

	Production				Income, Change in Domestic Credit, Debt Service, Wealth and Factor Endowment					Trade Flows		
	z_1	z_2	z_3	Y	ΔD	DS	W	K		e_1	$-e_2$	B
1952	502.07	501.98	1738.81	2878.61	5.73	8.96	14696.3	0.3465		102.96	97.74	5.22
1961	581.66	604.81	1698.80	3009.36	4.35	15.96	19889.9	0.3098		134.02	119.40	14.62
1971	831.76	799.24	2224.71	6516.82	43.00	22.72	32418.0	0.3438		273.53	292.73	-19.20
Sample Mean	655.95	659.54	1849.81	3834.21	13.32	15.63	21250.5	0.3307		157.79	153.69	4.10

[a]See Tables 5 and 6 for meaning of notation. Data sources are given in the appendix. The subscript 1 refers to exportables, 2 to importables, and 3 to nontraded goods. All variables (except prices) are expressed in per capita terms and the units of all values are current dollars per capita.

r_t to be constant over the sample period, and set it equal to its sample mean; we also include a constant term, denoted by κ, in this equation so that its residuals have a zero mean.[1]

With the three sector setup, there are 18 (= 6 + 4n with n = 3) endogenous variables. We can, however, drop one equation from LES since estimates of its parameters can be determined from the remaining two equations; we drop the exportables equation. In addition, the following endogenous variables can be dropped when estimating the model because they are all determined by identities, and these variables do not appear elsewhere in the system: v_i (i = 1, 2, 3), e_i (i = 1, 2), and B. Hence, in the truncated (but equivalent) model, there are eleven endogenous variables with six stochastic equations and five identities. The endogenous variables are A, absorption, C, consumption, W, wealth, v_2^c and v_3^c, consumption expenditure on importables and nontraded goods, respectively, P, the aggregate price index, z_i (i = 1, 2, 3), the domestic supply of each commodity, Y, income, and p_3, the price of nontraded goods. The predetermined variables are I, total investment expenditure, K, the aggregate resource endowment, ΔD, the change in the domestic credit component of high-powered money, DS, the debt service surplus, v_3^i, the value of investment demands for the output of the nontraded goods sector, p_1 and p_2, the price of exportables and importables, respectively, together with the lagged values of most of these variables, and the lagged endogenous variables.

We estimate the model under the restriction that ρ, the first order autoregressive parameter matrix in equation (3.3), is diagonal, with the diagonal elements denoted by ρ_i. This rules out autocorrelation across

---

[1]This "identity" has residuals merely because of the approximation in setting r equal to its mean.

equations. Also, we impose the further restriction that ρ_i's in LES take
the same value. This restriction is needed to preserve invariance of the
LES parameter estimates with respect to the choice of which equation is
deleted in estimation, when ρ is diagonal [see Berndt and Savin (1975)].

When initially estimating the model, the rate of convergence of
the supply parameters, the π_{ij}'s, was slow. We solve this problem in a
somewhat pragmatic fashion by setting the off-diagonal elements of the
Π-matrix equal to zero (since $\Phi = \Pi\Pi'$, Π diagonal means that Φ is also
diagonal). This means that the fitted transformation function is no longer
a flexible functional form. In fact, the associated supply system is quite
rigid: all own-price supply elasticities are less than unity, all commodities are gross substitutes in production, and the elasticity of supply
of good i with respect to the price of good j (i $\neq$ j) is independent of i.

In the aggregate price index identity, we set the θ's equal to
their initial estimates, which were obtained by estimating the model using
the GNP deflator for P.[1] The reason for doing this is that the P-series
was generated using these θ-estimates in equation (2.22), as mentioned
previously.

In Table 8, we give the maximum likelihood parameter estimates and
their asymptotic standard errors, derived from the information matrix. Here,
we use the following notation. The γ_i (i = 1, 2, 3) are the utility function parameters for exportables, importables, and nontraded goods; γ_4 is

---

[1]P was treated as an exogenous variable to obtain these initial
(FIML) estimates. The initial estimate of the θ-vector, with asymptotic
standard errors in parentheses, is

$$[0.07446 \qquad 0.28698 \qquad 0.63856],$$
$$(0.00871) \qquad (0.01574) \qquad (0.01743)$$

which is reasonably close to the final estimate, given below in Table 8.

TABLE 8

MAXIMUM LIKELIHOOD PARAMETER ESTIMATES[a]

Parameter	Estimate	Parameter	Estimate
γ_1[b]	289.15 (15.02)	ρ_2	1.01118 (0.00531)
γ_2[b]	697.88 (65.02)	ρ_3	0.98301 (0.03989)
γ_3[b]	1271.47 (122.80)	ρ_4	0.94912 (0.03480)
γ_4[b]	31463.51 (1767.31)	ρ_5	0.76243 (0.10648)
θ_1	0.06591 (0.01037)	κ_1	−18.56 (5.84)
θ_2	0.29778 (0.02024)	κ_2	−40.82 (7.94)
θ_3	0.63631 (0.02152)	κ_3	143.74 (51.33)
α	0.50746 (0.10396)	κ_4	−12.45
ϕ_1	0.06598 (0.10657)	κ_5	0.00243
ϕ_2	0.53186 (0.09667)	κ_6	3668.47
ϕ_3	0.40216 (0.04724)	κ_7	1817.21
ρ_1	0.78696 (0.04505)	--	--

[a]Asymptotic standard errors in parentheses. See text for meaning of notation.

[b]Units of the γ's are dollars per capita at sample mean prices.

the wealth utility function parameter; the θ_i (i = 1, 2, 3) are the marginal budget shares for the three commodities; α is the speed of adjustment parameter in the absorption equation; the ϕ_i (i = 1, 2, 3) are the diagonal elements of Φ, the supply parameter matrix; ρ_1 is the first order autoregressive parameter of the LES disturbances, ρ_2 the corresponding parameter in the absorption equation, and the ρ_i (i = 3, 4, 5) are the supply equation autocorrelation coefficients; finally, the κ_i (i = 1, . . . , 7) are the constant terms in the three supply equations, the wealth equation, the aggregate price index expression, the income equation, and the nontraded goods market clearing requirement. The constant terms in the "identities," the κ_i (i = 4, . . . , 7), are set at values such that the residuals of each have a zero mean.

As noted in Chapter II, since the γ's determine the origin of the Klein-Rubin utility function, they are sometimes interpreted as subsistence quantities (when positive), in the sense that the consumer enjoys utility from the consumption of good i only when $x_i > \gamma_i$.[1] Under this interpretation, at sample mean prices, the cost of per capita subsistence of exportables is \$289, importables \$698, and for nontraded goods the cost is \$1,271. As a percentage of mean expenditures, these costs are about 93, 89, and 83 percent, respectively. The total cost of subsistence represents approximately 86 percent of mean total consumption expenditure. These all appear to be too large for the subsistence interpretation to be plausible. In fact, the γ_1- and γ_2-estimates are so large that they exceed the quantity consumed of exportables and importables for the period 1952-1958. This represents a violation of the utility function specification

---

[1] See Chapter II for a qualification to this terminology.

and a partial weakness of the demand side of the model.[1] On the other hand,
the consumption of nontraded goods exceeds the γ_3-estimate for the entire
sample period.

The interpretation of γ_4 as subsistence real wealth holdings seems
somewhat more tenuous. It is best to view γ_4 as just a utility function
parameter, with no physical interpretation. The γ_4-estimate is also too
large in relation to wealth holdings in the sample period: real wealth
holdings are less than the γ_4-estimate in all years of our sample. This
parameter estimate is about 50 percent greater than mean per capital real
wealth holdings, and about 28 percent larger than wealth holdings in 1971,
the final year of the sample period.

All the γ-estimates are reasonably well determined: the lowest
ratio of a γ-estimate to its asymptotic standard error is about ten.

According to the estimated marginal budget shares, the θ's, a $100
increment in total consumption expenditure gives rise to an additional
$6.60 of domestic spending on exportables, $29.80 on importables, and
$63.60 on nontraded goods. These parameters are also estimates with
reasonable precision, with the lowest ratio of a θ-estimate to its asymptotic standard error being about six.

The estimate of α, the speed of adjustment parameter, means that
about one-half of the gap between actual and long-run desired wealth is
closed each year by total spending being greater or less than income. This

[1]The problem of large γ-estimates has arisen in previous applications of LES to U.S. data [Lluch and Williams (1975, p. 58) and Pollak and
Wales (1969, p. 622)]. In general, however, this problem does not seem to
arise with LES estimates for other countries: Lluch and Powell (1975) estimate LES for nineteen countries (both developed and less developed), and ex-
perience difficulties with large γ-estimates in only two cases (at sample
means), one of which is the U.S. when a maximum likelihood estimator is used
[Lluch and Powell (1975, p. 292)].

estimate is quite close to an adjustment parameter estimated by Jonson and
Danes (1976) for the U.S. In the Jonson–Danes model, the adjustment
parameter relates aggregate private demand to the gap between desired and
actual real cash balances. On the other hand, in relation to some of
Jonson's (1976) findings for the U.K., this represents a relatively rapid
movement to long-run equilibrium. The large–sample 95 percent confidence
interval for α is [0.30, 0.71], which is moderately narrow.

The values of the individual ϕ-estimates have no meaning by them-
selves due to the arbitrary normalization. Their relative values determine
the supply elasticities, which we discuss shortly. The estimate of ϕ_1 is
not significantly different from zero. On the other hand, the other two
ϕ-estimates are significantly different from zero--the ϕ_2-estimate is five
and a half standard errors away from zero, while the ϕ_3-estimate is eight
and a half.

All the estimates of the first order autoregressive parameters,
with the exception of the ρ_2-estimate, lie within the unit circle, as required for stability. There is some evidence that the estimate of ρ_2 is
greater than unity due to sampling variability (the parameter estimate is
only about two standard errors greater than one).

As a descriptive guide to the model's predictive ability, we give
a quasi-R^2 for each stochastic equation of the truncated model in Table 9.
We define this statistic as the proportion of the variance of an endogenous
variable explained by the structural form of the model. Also given in the
table is the quasi-R^2 for consumption expenditure on exportables (which is
dropped in the truncated version of the model). As can be seen from the
table, the demand equations tend to fit the data better than do the supply
equations.

TABLE 9

QUASI-R^2's[a]

Endogenous Variable	Quasi-R^2
Absorption	0.9951
Consumption Expenditure on Exportables	0.9927
Consumption Expenditure on Importables	0.9946
Consumption Expenditure on Nontraded Goods	0.9991
Supply of Exportables	0.9561
Supply of Importables	0.9466
Supply of Nontraded Goods	0.9789

[a]Quasi-$R_i^2 = 1 - \text{var}(\hat{v}_i)/\text{var}(y_i)$, where $\hat{v}_i$ is the residual of structural equation i, and y_i is the ith endogenous variable.

The structural demand elasticities, evaluated at sample means, are given in Table 10. These elasticities have the usual LES characteristics: there are no inferior goods, all commodities are gross complements and net substitutes, and all uncompensated own-price elasticities are less than unity in absolute value. In general, the price elasticities are low. The reason is that our three commodities represent very broad aggregates. By comparing the uncompensated with the corresponding compensated elasticities, it can be seen that income effects represent a large proportion of the uncompensated price responses. It is of some interest to note that the exportables expenditure elasticity is only a little over one-half the other two expenditure elasticities.

In Table 11 we give the structural supply elasticities, evaluated at sample means. The highest own-price elasticity is for exportables, being about twice the size of the other two. The reason why the two off-diagonal

TABLE 10

STRUCTURAL DEMAND ELASTICITIES

	Expenditure	Price[a]		
		1	2	3
1. Exportables	.5566	−.1238	−.1482	−.2699
		−.0579	.0185	.0394
2. Importables	.9938	−.1096	−.3709	−.4820
		.0069	−.0731	.0663
3. Nontraded Goods	1.0934	−.1206	−.2911	−.6904
		.0098	.0443	−.0541

[a]Line 1—uncompensated; line 2—compensated.

TABLE 11

STRUCTURAL SUPPLY ELASTICITIES

i	Elasticity of Supply of Good i with Respect to Price of Good j		
	1	2	3
1. Exportables	.9340	−.5319	−.4022
2. Importables	−.0660	.4681	−.4022
3. Nontraded Goods	−.0660	−.5319	.5978

elements of each column take the same value here is because Φ, the supply system parameter matrix, is restricted to be diagonal. This restriction also results in all goods being gross substitutes in production, and all own-price supply elasticities being less than unity, as is the case in Table 11, and as was noted previously.

To evaluate the ability of the estimated model to track the paths of the endogenous variables over the sample period, we simulate it dynamically.[1]

---

[1]We refer here to the operational model, set out in Table 4, with the Table 8 parameter estimates.

That is, to solve the model for the endogenous variables each period, we use the previous period's simulated values of the endogenous variables for the current period's lagged endogenous variables. The simulation program we use is PREDIC, written by Wymer (1974). The mean percentage errors and root mean square percentage errors for the endogenous variables of interest are given in Table 12. Also, in Figures 1 through 15, the actual and simulated values of these variables are plotted; here, the actual value is represented by a heavy line, and simulated by a light line.

With the notable exception of the trade balance, the model appears to capture the main characteristics of most of the endogenous variables reasonably well. With respect to the trade balance, the errors of the exports and imports equations (which, in turn, are related to the errors of the exportables and importables domestic demand and supply equations) do not offset each other. Expressing the difference between these two errors as a proportion of the trade balances, which is a relatively small magnitude, results in a huge percentage error. This is a somewhat disappointing feature of the model. On the other hand, however, its ability to track the trade balance is probably a particularly stringent test of the model. The reason is twofold. First, the trade balance is a function of all the other endogenous variables of the model, and hence its simulated values can reflect all the simulation errors in these variables, i.e., if the errors do not offset each other. Second, over the sample period, of all the endogenous variables, the trade balance has by far the highest coefficient of variation (it is 2.7), indicating that it is possibly inherently difficult to predict.

The model does somewhat better in tracking the components of the trade balance, exports and imports. Their RMSPE's, however, are quite high in relation to that of the other variables--30 percent for exports and 23

TABLE 12

MEAN PERCENTAGE ERRORS AND ROOT MEAN SQUARE PERCENTAGE
ERRORS: DYNAMIC SIMULATION OVER SAMPLE PERIOD

Endogenous Variable	MPE[a]	RMSPE[b]
Absorption	.02107	.03950
Total Consumption Expenditure	.02578	.04833
Wealth	.02778	.03822
Consumption Expenditure on Exportables	.009153	.01718
Consumption Expenditure on Importables	.02386	.03959
Consumption Expenditure on Nontraded Goods	.02888	.06815
Aggregate Price Index	.009136	.02172
Supply of Exportables	.02464	.06817
Supply of Importables	.01968	.05345
Supply of Nontraded Goods	.01160	.02032
Income	.03238	.08473
Value of Exports	.1009	.2977
Value of Imports	.03149	.2250
Price of Nontraded Goods	.01273	.03579
Trade Balance	36.98	143.3

[a]$MPE_i = \frac{1}{T} \sum_{t=1}^{T} (y_{it}^s - y_{it})/y_{it}$, in which

y_i^s is the simulated value of endogenous variable i, and

y_i is the actual value of the ith endogenous variable.

[b]$RMSPE_i = \{\frac{1}{T} \sum_{t=1}^{T} [(y_{it}^s - y_{it})/y_{it}]^2\}^{1/2}$.

percent for imports. This again is due to the fact that these are excess
supplies, and the errors cumulate.

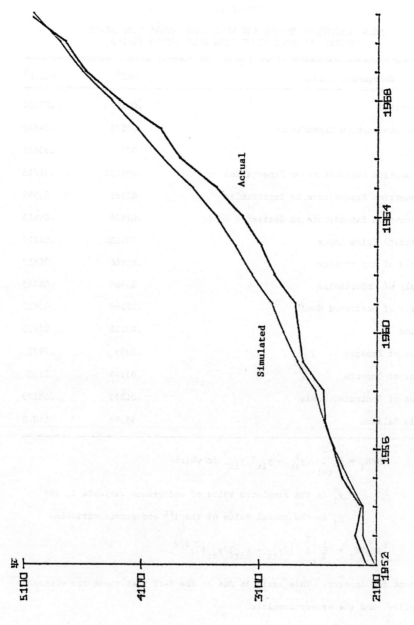

Fig. 1.—Absorption: Actual and simulated.

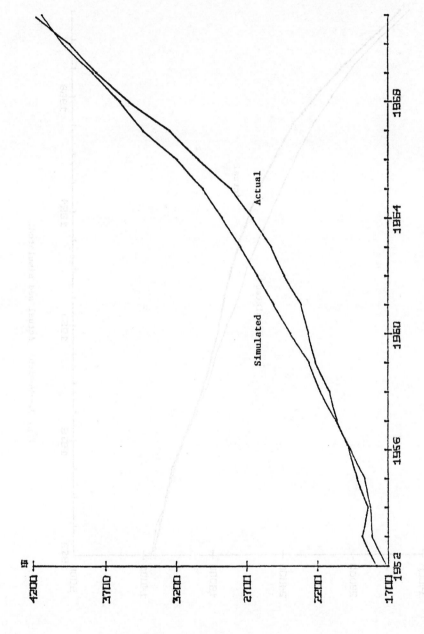

Fig. 2.—Total consumption expenditure: Actual and simulated

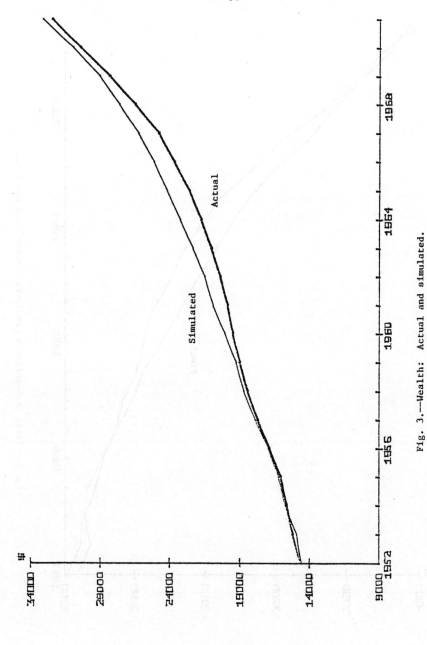

Fig. 3.—Wealth: Actual and simulated.

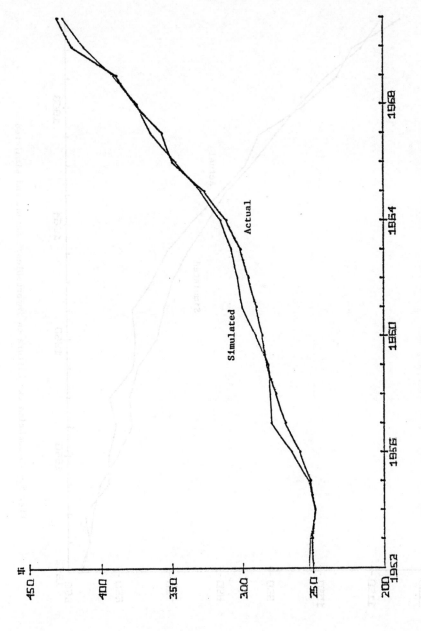

Fig. 4.—Consumption expenditure on exportables: Actual and simulated

60

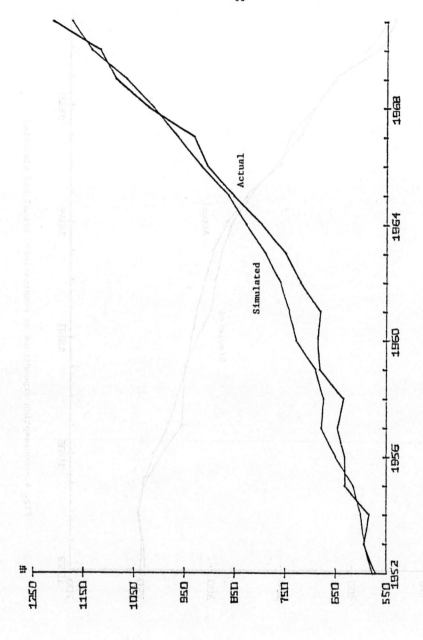

Fig. 5.—Consumption expenditure on importables: Actual and simulated

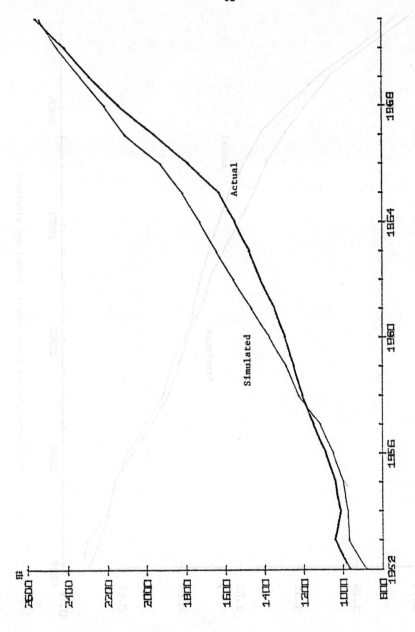

Fig. 6.—Consumption expenditure on nontraded goods: Actual and simulated

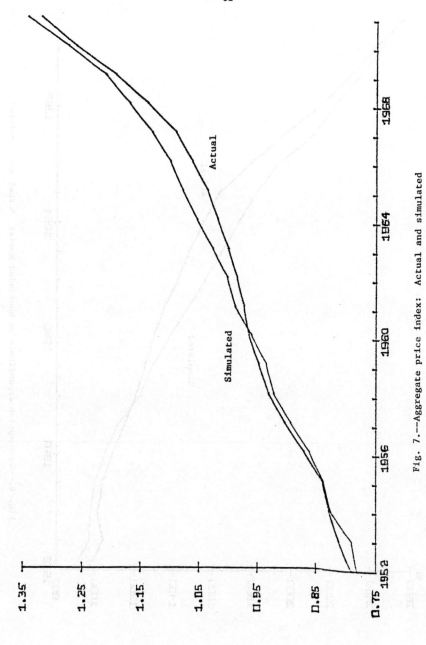

Fig. 7.--Aggregate price index: Actual and simulated

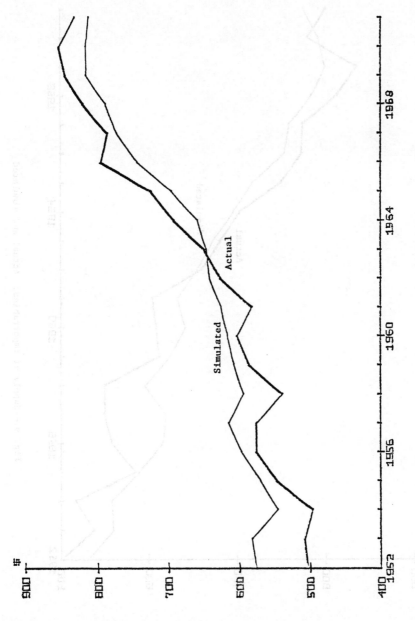

Fig. 8.--Supply of exportables: Actual and simulated

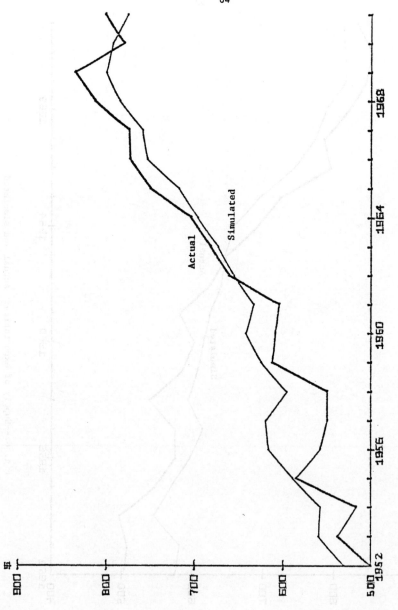

Fig. 9.--Supply of importables: Actual and simulated

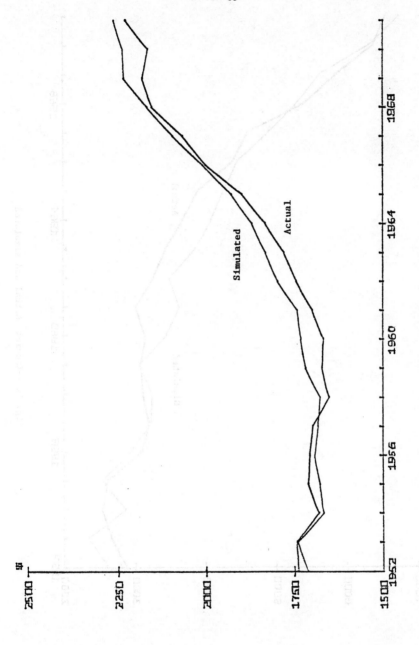

Fig. 10.--Supply of nontraded goods: Actual and simulated

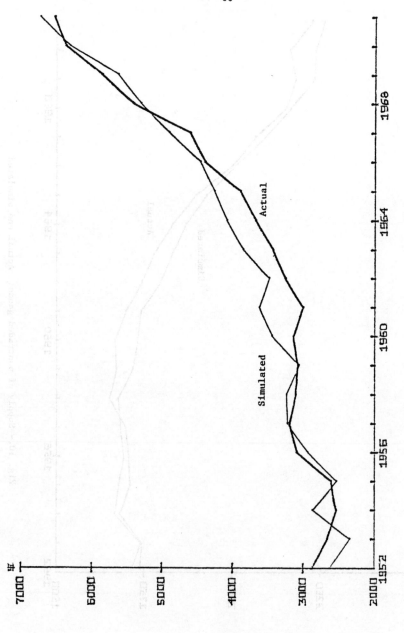

Fig. 11.--Income: Actual and simulated

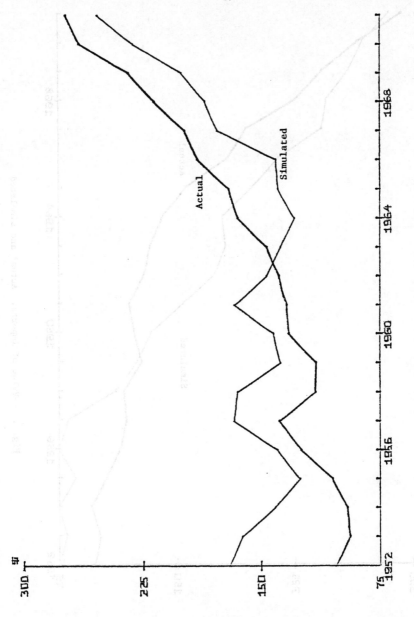

Fig. 12.--Value of exports: Actual and simulated

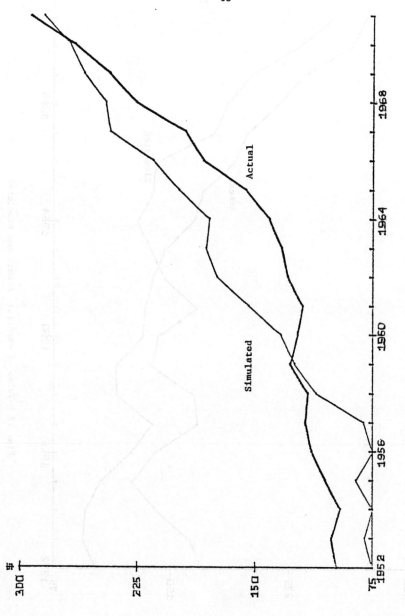

Fig. 13.--Value of imports: Actual and simulated

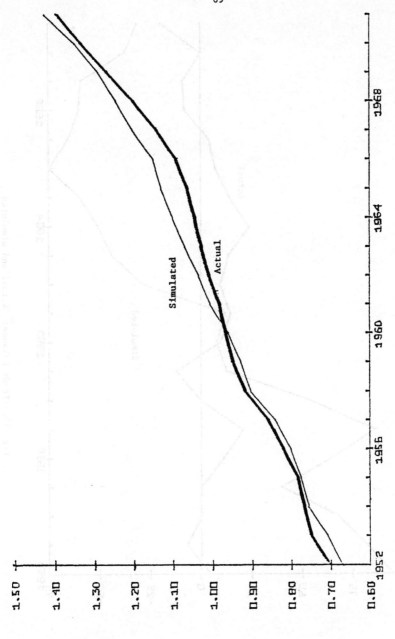

Fig. 14.--Price of nontraded goods: Actual and simulated

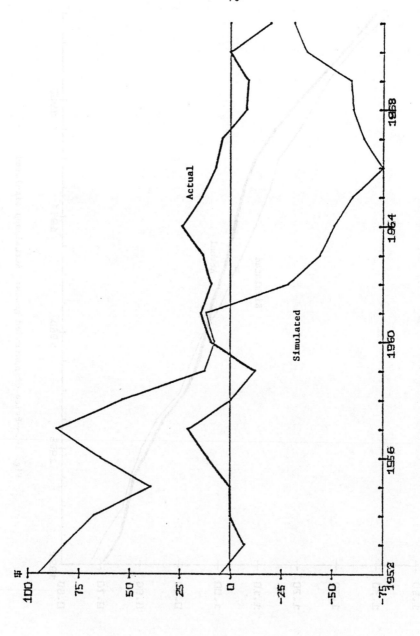

Fig. 15.--Trade balance: Actual and simulated

Concluding Comments

      In this chapter, we have made the theoretical model of the previous chapter operational and have estimated its parameters with U.S. data. The empirical results are encouraging. However, some problems remain. First, most of the estimated γ-parameters of the Klein-Rubin utility function tend to be too large, a problem which has come up previously. Second, the fitted supply system is quite rigid. Third, the model is not capable of tracking the path of the trade balance over the sample period.

      In the empirical implementation, the U.S. is treated as a small open economy, allowing us to take the prices of traded goods as exogenous. Due to its large size, the U.S. may in fact, however, have some short-run monopoly power in international trade, causing the traded commodities prices to be endogenous. Hence, this may be a potential limitation of the empirical results. Although the application of the model to the U.S. may not fully satisfy the assumptions of the model, it may nevertheless be viewed as an illustrative application of a framework which is readily applicable to other countries.

CHAPTER IV

APPLICATIONS: DEVALUATION, TARIFFS AND
DOMESTIC MONETARY EXPANSION

Introduction

In this chapter, we use the estimated model in three policy experiments for the U.S. The model is used to simulate the effects on the endogenous variables of a devaluation, the imposition of a tariff on imports, and an increase in the rate of growth of domestic credit. These policy changes are fictitious in the sense that they did not actually occur during sample period.

The effects of the policy changes are isolated by comparing the new solution to the model with the control solution. The former is obtained by solving the model each period using the previous period's simulated values of the endogenous variables for this period's lagged endogenous variables, the new exogenous variables associated with the hypothetical policy change, and the actual values of the remaining exogenous variables. The control solution is obtained by solving the model dynamically with the actual values of all the exogenous variables. This control solution is identical to that used in the previous chapter to evaluate the tracking ability of the model--it is represented by the "simulated" series in Figures 1 through 15, pp. 56-70.

Comparing the two solutions in this way means that we are not comparing the new solution with the actual paths of the endogenous variables,

72

but with the paths predicted by the model when all the exogenous variables take their actual values. This means that we are abstracting from the simulation errors—the difference between simulated and actual values—discussed in Chapter III. This procedure also means that these experiments are essentially _ceteris paribus_ in the following sense. Changes in the other exogenous variables of the model have a common effect on both solutions, and, hence, the difference between the two solutions solely reflects the effects of the policy change.

All policy shocks take place in 1959, and we give the new time paths of the endogenous variables of interest for the period 1959 to 1971. The reason for using 1959 is that this is the first year in which the consumption of each commodity exceeds its estimated γ-parameter, as was discussed in the previous chapter. It is only then that all own-price demand elasticities are negative.

The simulation program we use is again PREDIC, written by Wymer (1974).

The chapter is structured as follows. First, we simulate a devaluation; second, a tariff; third, the domestic monetary expansion; and fourth, we give some concluding comments.

Devaluation

In the model, devaluation is represented by an increase in the domestic price of the traded goods which is equi-proportional to the devaluation. This is because, for a small country, the world prices of these goods are parametric, unaffected by the devaluation. We thus abstract from short-run deviations from the purchasing power parity for traded goods.

Devaluation has two effects in the model. First, there is an initial change in the prices of the traded goods relative to the nontraded goods, and this causes long-run desired wealth to change. This results in a gap between actual and desired wealth, which is closed gradually by spending differing from income. From the budget constraint, this means that, in the transition period, the trade balance will change. Over time, actual wealth is brought into line with the desired stock, and, in full equilibrium, they are equal; here, spending again equals income, the current account is zero, and there will be no change in the trade balance.[1]

The second effect of devaluation is a transient change in both the production and consumption pattern caused by the relative price change. The devaluation induced relative price change will, however, tend to be reversed over time. The mechanism by which this takes place is that spending differs from income, and this pushes up the nontraded goods price. If the full equilibrium position of the economy is unique, we would expect the devaluation to have no permanent effect on relative prices. This follows from the property of the model of homogeneity of degree zero in all nominal variables. Hence, in the long run, devaluation has no real effects.[2] The reason why there are real short-run effects of devaluation, or, in other words, the reason why relative price change at all, is that initially spending differs from income.

---

[1] Recent monetary model of devaluation [e.g., Dornbusch (1973a, 1973b, 1974), Frenkel and Rodriguez (1975), and Johnson (1976a, 1976b)] emphasize an alternative mechanism by which spending differs from income over the adjustment period. Devaluation raises the domestic price level, causing real cash balances to fall. Holdings of real balances are gradually restored to their previous level by hoarding part of income, and running a trade balance surplus (in the simplest versions of these models). Such a real balance effect is not present in our model because we specify that all wealth is denominated in real terms.

[2] On the long-run neutrality of devaluation, see, e.g., Dornbusch (1973a, 1974) and Mundell (1968, Chap. VIII).

These two effects of devaluation might be termed an expenditure-changing effect and an expenditure-switching effect [cf. Johnson (1958)].

We simulate a 10 percent unilateral devaluation in 1959 by increasing the actual domestic prices of both exportables and importables by 10 percent for the period 1959 to 1971. Also, we increase the actual debt service surplus by 10 percent for the same period. This amounts to specifying that all domestic holdings of foreign securities are denominated in terms of foreign currency.

It should be noted that we are partly abstracting from the associated capital gain on domestic holdings of foreign securities. That is, the value of the foreign security holdings in terms of the domestic currency increases by the same percentage as the devaluation. We do, however, take account of these capital gains to the extent that the domestic price level rises as a result of the devaluation. This is because we specify that real wealth is invariant to changes in the price level, and as a result, in the income definition [equation (2.29)] we have the term $\hat{P}W$, the increase in the nominal value of wealth due to a rise in the price level, and included in W are holdings of foreign securities. It is unlikely that the domestic price level would rise by the full amount of devaluation contemporaneously; it is more likely that only after some time will the price level rise by the full amount. Hence, the error involved in using this procedure is likely to be one of timing of the capital gain on the foreign securities: our procedure probably shows the full capital gain sometime after the devaluation.

In Figures 16 through 19, we plot the devaluation simulated and the control values of the endogenous variables of interest. Also, in Table 13, for three of these variables we give the simulated value as a percentage of

76

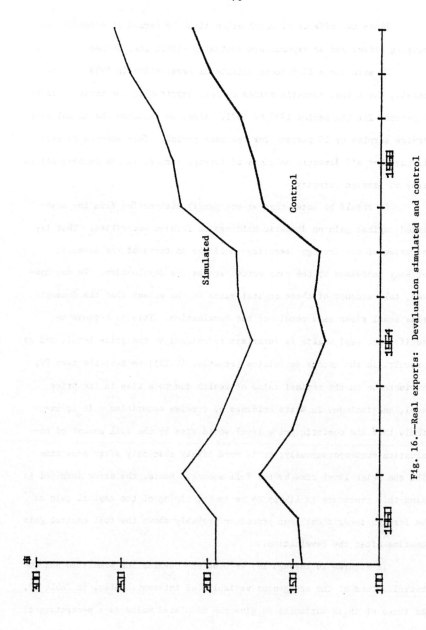

Fig. 16.—Real exports: Devaluation simulated and control

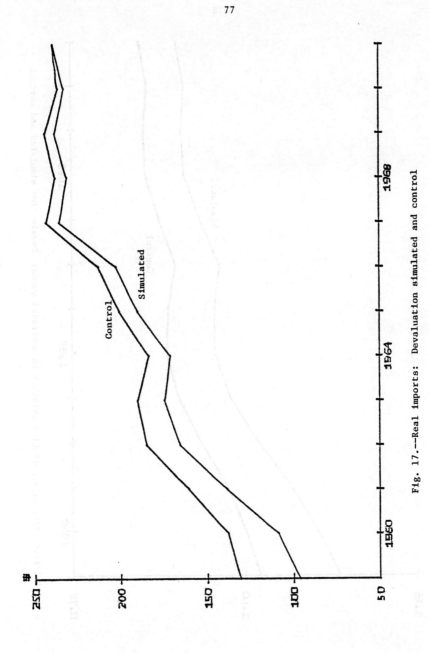

Fig. 17.—Real imports: Devaluation simulated and control

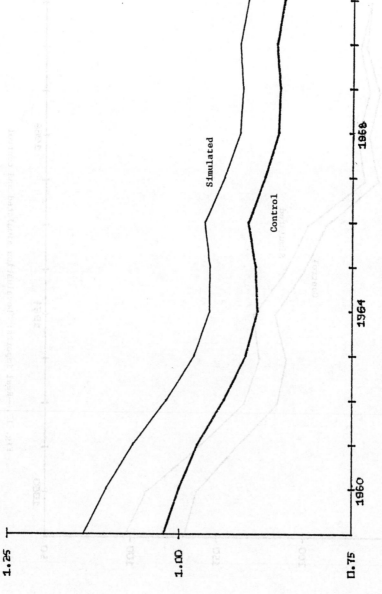

Fig. 18.--Price of exportables relative to nontraded goods: Devaluation simulated and control

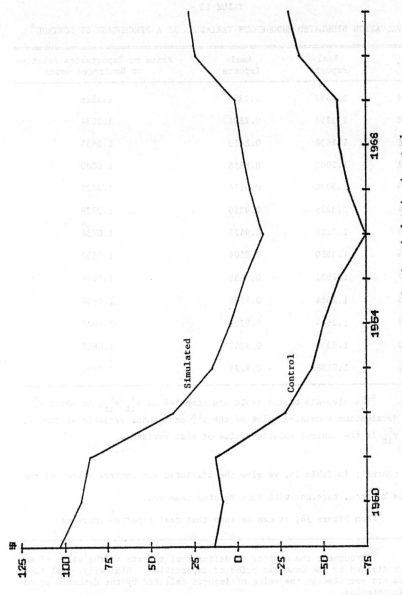

Fig. 19.—Trade balance: Devaluation simulated and control

TABLE 13

DEVALUATION SIMULATED ENDOGENOUS VARIABLES AS A PERCENTAGE OF CONTROL[a]

Year	Real Exports	Real Imports	Price of Exportables Relative to Nontraded Goods
1959	1.3467	0.7357	1.1126
1960	1.3236	0.7884	1.1034
1961	1.2634	0.8613	1.0951
1962	1.2963	0.8956	1.0880
1963	1.3030	0.9174	1.0825
1964	1.3229	0.9320	1.0779
1965	1.3228	0.9472	1.0736
1966	1.3580	0.9509	1.0697
1967	1.2831	0.9683	1.0666
1968	1.2684	0.9709	1.0644
1969	1.2644	0.9759	1.0625
1970	1.2337	0.9847	1.0615
1971	1.2158	0.9979	1.0609

[a]The elements of the table are computed as y_{it}^s/y_{it}^c, in which y_{it}^s is the devaluation simulated value of the ith endogenous variable at time t, and y_{it}^c is the control solution value of that variable.

the control; in Table 14, we give the simulated and control values of the trade balance, together with some related measures.

From Figure 16, it can be seen that real exports[1] increase

[1]Throughout the chapter we define real exports as the value of exports divided by the domestic price of exportables. Similarly, real imports are computed as the value of imports deflated by the domestic price of importables.

TABLE 14

TRADE BALANCE: DEVALUATION SIMULATED AND CONTROL[a]

Year	B^S	B^C	$B^S - B^C$	$(B^S - B^C)/|B^C|$
1959	103.13	13.11	90.02	6.8665
1960	90.54	8.29	82.25	9.9216
1961	85.14	12.24	72.90	5.9559
1962	37.04	−27.90	64.94	2.3276
1963	14.35	−43.60	57.95	1.3291
1964	3.55	−50.53	54.08	1.0703
1965	−4.59	−59.44	54.85	0.9228
1966	−15.55	−74.80	59.25	0.7921
1967	−8.25	−65.29	57.04	0.8736
1968	−3.44	−59.96	56.52	0.9426
1969	0.27	−58.90	59.13	1.0046
1970	22.82	−37.25	60.07	1.6126
1971	26.66	−31.03	57.69	1.8592

[a]B^S is the devaluation simulated value of the trade balance, and B^C is the control solution value. Units are current dollars per capita.

substantially during the year of the devaluation; from Table 13, real exports increase by about 35 percent as a result of the devaluation. Although there is a tendency for this increase to die out over time, the rate of decay is low, and twelve years after the devaluation in 1971, exports are still approximately 22 percent larger than they would otherwise be. Hence, the speed of adjustment of the system as a whole is slow.[1]

---

[1]In Chapter III, we noted that the estimate of α, the speed of

To be contrasted with exports, is the behavior of real imports.
From Figure 17, imports fall somewhat as a result of the devaluation.
Over time, however, they rise back to what they would have otherwise been:
by 1965, six years after the devaluation they are about 95 percent of what
imports would otherwise be, while by 1971 they are approximately the same
as the control value.

The behavior of the time path of the domestic price of exportables
relative to nontraded goods, plotted in Figure 18, displays some interesting characteristics. In the year of the devaluation and the year following,
there is some overshooting of this price: its percentage increase is more
than the devaluation (see Table 13), indicating that the nontraded goods
price actually falls relative to the control in the initial two years.
The reason for this fall is that the expenditure-reducing effect of the
devaluation outweighs the expenditure-switching effect. This overshooting
is reversed two years after the devaluation. This relative price falls
continuously following the devaluation and twelve years later it is about
6 percent higher than otherwise. Again the speed of adjustment to long-
run equilibrium which, in this case, is represented by no change in relative prices, as discussed above, seems to be slow.

Devaluation has the effect of improving the trade balance, and, as
can be seen from Figure 19 and Table 14, the improvement is most marked in
the first three years. Following that period, devaluation still improves
the trade balance and the absolute improvement is of about the same order
of magnitude. There is some tendency for the improvement to display a

---

adjustment parameter in the absorption equation, implies a relatively rapid
movement to long-run equilibrium. This, however, is a partial statement
since it refers to one equation only of the system. The dynamics of the
model are also generated by the autoregressive disturbance term in each
stochastic equation.

cyclical pattern commencing around 1966. This probably means that the system has a complex characteristic root.

The long-run effect of devaluation on the trade balance should be zero, as discussed above. The Table 14 results do not either support or refute this prediction. We can, however, make the following summary statement. The beneficial effect of devaluation on the trade balance does indeed fall over time, but the lags appear to be very long.

In conclusion, the results for the trade balance should probably be treated with due care, given the basic inability of the estimated model to track the actual path of this variable over the sample period, as noted in the previous chapter. This caveat also applies to the trade balance simulations in the following two sections.

A Tariff on Imports

The imposition of a tariff on imports is represented by an increase in the domestic price of importables which is equi-proportional to the tariff rate. This also has two effects in the model. First, as with the devaluation, the change in relative prices induces a difference between spending and income in the short run, which, in turn, implies a change in both the current account and the balance of trade. In the long run, income equals spending and there will be no change in the trade balance resulting from the tariff, as before.

The second effect is that the tariff results in a permanent change in relative prices, and this has real effects even in the long run. The increase in the domestic price of importables relative to exportables induces an increase in the domestic output of the importables sector and a fall in the production of exportables. The resulting change in the domestic consumption pattern is in the opposite direction to the production change.

84

These two effects reenforce each other to give the unambiguous result that both exports and imports fall.

We simulate a 10 percent tariff in 1959 by increasing the actual domestic price of importables by 10 percent for the period 1959-1971. We neglect the tariff revenue because it is trivial in relation to income.[1]

We plot in Figures 20 through 23 the tariff simulated and the control values of the endogenous variables of interest. Also, in Table 15, for three of these variables we give the simulated value as a percentage of the control; the simulated and control values of the trade balance and some related measures are given in Table 16.[2]

The tariff lowers real exports by about 20 percent in all periods. We can obtain the elasticity of exports with respect to the domestic price of importables by subtracting unity from Column 2 of Table 15 to give the percentage change in exports and then dividing this by 0.1, the percentage increase in the importables price. Thus, for example, the contemporaneous elasticity is -1.614, while the twelve year elasticity[3] is -1.891. These are reduced form elasticities in the sense that no endogenous variables of the model are held constant.

From Figure 21, it can be seen that the tariff induces a substantial reduction in real imports. The impact effect on imports is the largest: imports fall by about 47 percent in the same year as the tariff

---

[1]From Table 7, at sample means, imports are about 4 percent of income. An upper estimate of the tariff revenue is obtained if we assume a zero price elasticity of demand for imports; this yields the result that the proceeds of a 10 percent tariff is only 0.4 percent of income.

[2]The control value of the trade balance in Table 16 is the same as the control value given in Table 14; it is repeated for convenience.

[3]That is, the ratio of the percentage change in exports twelve years after the imposition of the tariff to the percentage change in the importables price when the tariff is imposed (viz., the tariff rate).

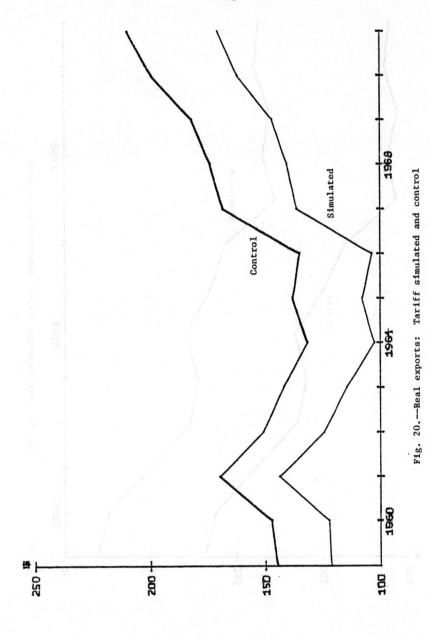

Fig. 20.—Real exports: Tariff simulated and control

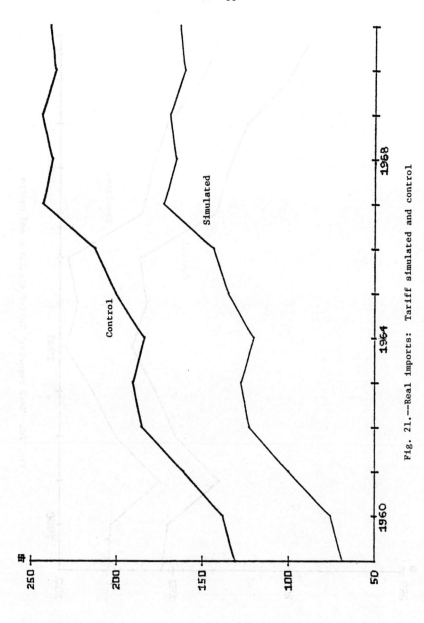

Fig. 21.--Real imports: Tariff simulated and control

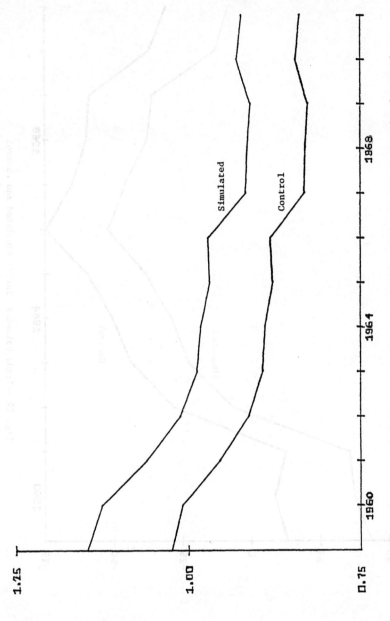

87

Fig. 22.—Price of importables relative to nontraded goods: Tariff simulated and control

88

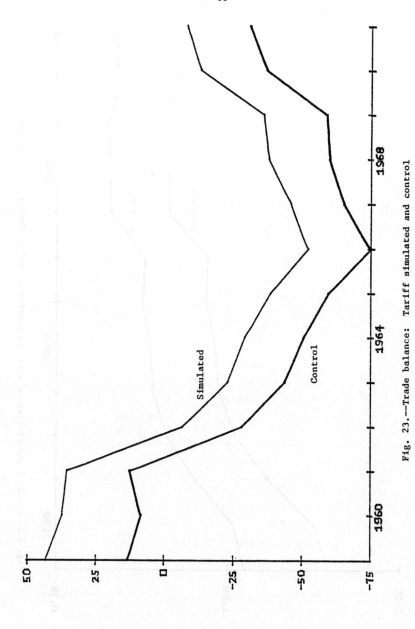

Fig. 23.--Trade balance: Tariff simulated and control

TABLE 15

TARIFF SIMULATED ENDOGENOUS VARIABLES AS A PERCENTAGE OF CONTROL[a]

Year	Real Exports	Real Imports	Price of Importables Relative to Nontraded Goods
1959	0.8386	0.5260	1.1191
1960	0.8304	0.5483	1.1158
1961	0.8470	0.6218	1.1121
1962	0.8247	0.6639	1.1091
1963	0.8062	0.6707	1.1070
1964	0.7796	0.6557	1.1053
1965	0.7812	0.6730	1.1037
1966	0.7668	0.6741	1.1023
1967	0.8098	0.7100	1.1007
1968	0.8075	0.6952	1.0999
1969	0.8077	0.6935	1.0992
1970	0.8118	0.6801	1.0991
1971	0.8109	0.6834	1.0988

[a]See Table 13 for definitions.

is imposed, while after twelve years imports are approximately 32 percent lower than they would otherwise be. The reduce form elasticity of imports with respect to their price can be computed in the same way as before: the contemporaneous elasticity is -4.74, while the twelve year elasticity is -3.166. These are quite reasonable magnitudes; they are, however, somewhat larger in absolute value than previous estimates for the U.S. [Magee (1975, p. 182)].

The domestic price of importables relative to nontraded goods,

90

TABLE 16

TRADE BALANCE: TARIFF SIMULATED AND CONTROL[a]

Year	B^s	B^c	$B^s - B^c$	$(B^s - B^c)/|B^c|$
1959	43.39	13.11	30.28	2.3097
1960	37.17	8.29	28.88	3.4837
1961	35.49	12.24	23.25	1.8995
1962	- 6.56	-27.90	21.34	0.7649
1963	-22.75	-43.60	20.85	0.4782
1964	-28.94	-50.53	21.59	0.4273
1965	-38.33	-59.44	21.11	0.3551
1966	-51.93	-74.80	22.87	0.3057
1967	-45.88	-65.29	19.41	0.2973
1968	-37.93	-59.96	22.03	0.3674
1969	-35.96	-58.90	22.94	0.3895
1970	-13.18	-37.25	24.07	0.6462
1971	- 8.32	-31.03	22.71	0.7319

[a]B^s is the tariff simulated value of the trade balance, and B^c is the control solution value. Units are current dollars per capita.

plotted in Figure 22, displays the same overshooting phenomena, before it settles down to a value greater than control by about the exact amount of the tariff.

The tariff improves the trade balance, and, as can be seen from Figure 23 and Table 16, it has its most marked effect in the first three years, as before. As in the devaluation case, we do not observe the zero long-run effect of the tariff on the trade balance--apparently the system takes longer than twelve years to reach the steady state position.

Domestic Monetary Expansion

The effect of domestic monetary expansion, or, more precisely, domestic credit expansion, is to raise income directly. This is because new high-powered money gets into the system via direct transfers [refer to the definition of income, equation (2.29)]. This means that spending on all goods increases according to the marginal budget shares. That is, all demand curves shift up and to the right. As a result, exports fall (as more exportables are consumed domestically) and imports increase, giving rise to an unambiguous deterioration of the trade balance on this count.

This result can also be seen from equation (2.32), the expression for the trade balance. The value of output $(Y - \dot{D} - \hat{P}W)$ can be taken as approximately constant for this analysis, so that an increase in the rate of growth of the domestic credit component of the monetary base, through its direct effect on income (in contrast to the value of output), raises spending, which in equation (2.32) is represented by C, consumption. Hence, monetary expansion raises spending relative to the value of output, and this induces a trade balance deficit.

There is a further effect of monetary policy on the trade balance. In the short run, monetary expansion is likely to push up the price of non-traded goods relative to the traded goods. This is due to the upward shift in the nontraded goods demand curve. This induces a change in the long-run desired stock of wealth, and a change in saving during the transition period, in which actual and desired wealth are brought into equality. As before, this change in saving results in a change in the current account and the trade balance, from the budget constraint.

In this simulation, we ignore the likely longer-run consequences of domestic monetary expansion. We ignore the fact that a sustained rate of

growth of domestic credit in the U.S. which is higher than that of the
rest of the world is most likely to lead to a continual depletion of international reserves. Hence, such a divergent domestic monetary policy is
just not feasible in the long run.

We simulate an expansion in the stock of the domestic credit component of the monetary base for the period 1959-1971 by doubling each
year's actual increase. In Table 17, we give the actual and simulated
values of the increase in domestic credit over this period, together with
the corresponding rates of growth. The actual rate of growth in the per
capita stock of domestic credit ranges from a low of about 0.6 percent per
annum in 1961 to a high of about 11 percent in 1971. The lowest rate of
growth in the per capita simulated stock is about 2 percent in 1961, while
the largest is approximately 15 percent in 1960.

We plot in Figures 24 through 27 the monetary expansion simulated
and the control values of the endogenous variables of interest. Also, in
Table 18, for three of these variables we give the simulated value as a
percentage of control, while the simulated and control values of the trade
balance are given in Table 19.[1]

From Table 18, the largest fall in exports in any one year as a result of the monetary expansion is about 2.5 percent. The percentage fall
tends to grow over time.

The percentage increase in imports as a result of the monetary expansion tends also to grow each year. In 1971, imports are about 5 percent
greater than they would otherwise be.

As can be seen from the fourth column of Table 18, the resulting

---

[1]The control solution value of the trade balance is repeated again
in Table 19 for convenience.

93

TABLE 17

SIMULATED AND CONTROL DOMESTIC CREDIT[a]

Year	ΔD^s	g^s	ΔD^c	g^c
1959	16.94	0.0798	8.47	0.0325
1960	33.20	0.1493	16.60	0.0723
1961	8.70	0.0237	4.35	0.0063
1962	31.06	0.1194	15.53	0.0643
1963	27.46	0.0929	13.73	0.0523
1964	36.44	0.1142	18.22	0.0691
1965	41.12	0.1161	20.56	0.0745
1966	52.82	0.1344	26.41	0.0916
1967	53.24	0.1187	26.62	0.0842
1968	38.86	0.0778	19.43	0.0568
1969	24.66	0.0414	12.33	0.0295
1970	51.74	0.0901	25.87	0.0679
1971	86.00	0.1392	43.00	0.1095

[a] ΔD is the change in the domestic credit component of the monetary base. The "s" superscript denotes the assumed value for the simulation, while the "c" superscript denotes the actual value (the control value). Units of ΔD are current dollars per capita.

g is the annual rate of growth of the per capita stock of domestic credit, i.e.,

$$g_t = \ln \left[\frac{D_t/N_t}{D_{t-1}/N_{t-1}}\right],$$

where N is population. The "s" superscript again refers to the simulated value, and the "c" to the control.

94

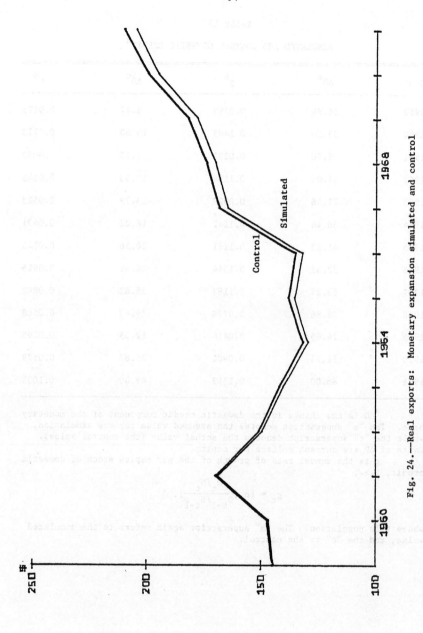

Fig. 24.—Real exports: Monetary expansion simulated and control

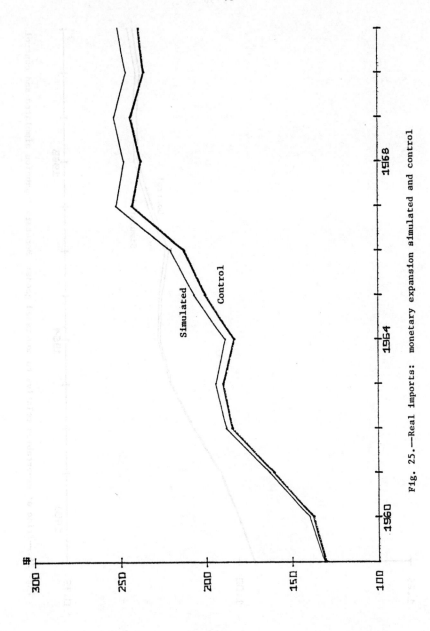

Fig. 25.—Real imports: monetary expansion simulated and control

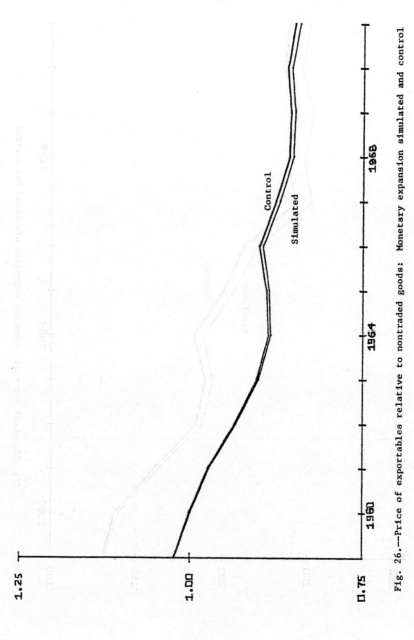

Fig. 26.—Price of exportables relative to nontraded goods: Monetary expansion simulated and control

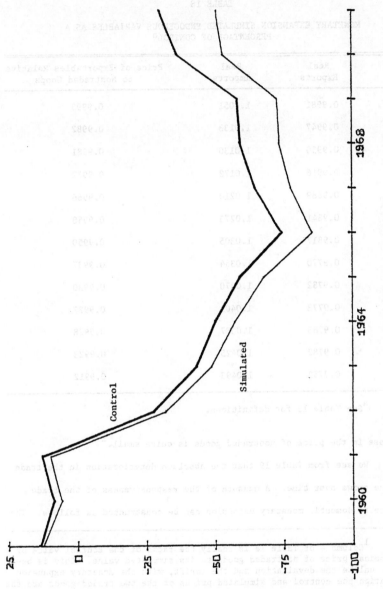

Fig. 27.--Trade balance: Monetary expansion simulated and control

TABLE 18

MONETARY EXPANSION SIMULATED ENDOGENOUS VARIABLES AS A
PERCENTAGE OF CONTROL[a]

Year	Real Exports	Real Imports	Price of Exportables Relative to Nontraded Goods
1959	0.9981	1.0051	0.9993
1960	0.9947	1.0138	0.9982
1961	0.9950	1.0130	0.9981
1962	0.9916	1.0172	0.9972
1963	0.9889	1.0210	0.9966
1964	0.9841	1.0273	0.9958
1965	0.9817	1.0305	0.9950
1966	0.9770	1.0354	0.9937
1967	0.9782	1.0370	0.9930
1968	0.9773	1.0401	0.9927
1969	0.9783	1.0387	0.9928
1970	0.9782	1.0425	0.9923
1971	0.9752	1.0493	0.9912

[a]See Table 13 for definitions.

increase in the price of nontraded goods is quite small.[1]

We see from Table 19 that the absolute deterioration in the trade balance grows over time. A measure of the responsiveness of the trade balance to domestic monetary expansion can be constructed as follows. The

[1]Column 4 of Table 18 is really the ratio of the control value of the nominal price of nontraded goods to its simulated value. This is because, unlike the devaluation and the tariff, with the monetary expansion simulation the control and simulated prices of the two traded goods are the same.

TABLE 19

TRADE BALANCE: MONETARY EXPANSION SIMULATED AND CONTROL[a]

Year	B^s	B^c	$B^s - B^c$	$(B^s - B^c)/|B^c|$
1959	12.21	13.11	- 0.90	-0.0686
1960	5.70	8.29	- 2.59	-0.3124
1961	9.39	12.24	- 2.85	-0.2328
1962	-32.15	-27.90	- 4.25	-0.1523
1963	-48.92	-43.60	- 5.32	-0.1220
1964	-57.46	-50.53	- 6.93	-0.1371
1965	-68.03	-59.44	- 8.59	-0.1445
1966	-85.63	-74.80	-10.83	-0.1448
1967	-78.12	-65.29	-12.83	-0.1965
1968	-73.99	-59.96	-14.03	-0.2340
1969	-73.26	-58.90	-14.36	-0.2438
1970	-53.65	-37.25	-16.40	-0.4403
1971	-51.32	-31.03	-20.29	-0.6539

[a]B^s is the monetary expansion simulated value of the trade balance, and B^c is the control solution value. Units are current dollars per capita.

per capita increment in the change in the domestic credit component of the monetary base summed over the thirteen years[1] is $251.12 (from Table 17). The deterioration in the per capita trade balance due to the additional

---

[1]That is,

$$\sum_{t=1}^{13} (\Delta D_t^s - \Delta D_t^c),$$

where the notation follows Table 17.

credit summed over the thirteen years[1] is $120.17. The ratio of these two quantities (the latter to the former) gives a rough guide to the responsiveness of the trade balance to an expansionary domestic credit policy. This ratio is about 0.48. Hence, over the thirteen years, approximately 48 percent of the additional credit gets translated into a deterioration of the trade balance.

In conclusion, it should be pointed out again that we use the level of employment as the aggregate resource endowment index, which is taken as exogenous. As a result, the model rules out any effect of domestic credit policy on employment. This may be a potential limitation of these monetary expansion simulation results.

Concluding Comments

In this chapter, the estimated model has been used for three policy simulations. We simulated the effects on exports, imports, the trade balance, and the price of nontraded goods in the U.S. of a 10 percent devaluation, a 10 percent tariff on imports, and an expansionary domestic credit policy.

Key findings for the devaluation are:

1. There is a substantial increase in exports. This increase tends to die out slowly.

2. Imports fall as a result of the devaluation, but increase back to what they would otherwise be moderately quickly.

---

[1]That is,

$$- \sum_{t=1}^{13} (B_t^s - B_t^c),$$

where the notation follows Table 19.

3. Following the devaluation, the adjustment of relative prices to what they would otherwise be is very slow.

4. The trade balance improves. The improvement is most marked in the first three years. After that, the improvement dies out very slowly, if at all.

Key findings for the imposition of the 10 percent tariff are:

1. Exports are permanently lowered by about 20 percent.

2. Imports are also permanently lowered.

3. There is some initial overshooting of the domestic price of importables relative to nontraded goods.

4. The tariff improves the balance of trade most markedly in the first three years following its imposition. Adjustment lags seem to be long.

Finally, key findings for the expansionary domestic credit policy are:

1. Exports fall and imports rise.

2. The trade balance deteriorates. About 48 percent of the additional credit gets translated into a deterioration of the balance of trade over a thirteen year period.

CHAPTER V

SUMMARY AND CONCLUSIONS

In this dissertation, we developed a simple multisector general
equilibrium model of the open economy. The parameters of the model were
then estimated with U.S. data. Finally, some of its uses were illustrated
by studying the effects of changes in three key policy variables: we
simulated a 10 percent devaluation of the U.S. dollar, the imposition of
a 10 percent tariff on imports, and an expansionary monetary policy.

The model is deliberately kept simple in order to facilitate,
first, an understanding of its workings, and, second, the empirical implementation. Nevertheless, the model is so simple that a word about its
potential limitations is probably required. First, there is no explicit
treatment of factor markets. Second, the role of expectations is somewhat
suppressed by the assumption of static expectations. Finally, because we
use employment as the measure of the aggregate factor endowment index,
which is taken as exogenous, the model does not allow for endogenous unemployment. Potentially, these all may be limitations of this study.

This study represents the first econometric application of a model
of this type. Moreover, we use relatively high-powered estimation tech-
niques to implement the model. Hence, the difficulties which we ex-
perienced in the empirical work are probably to be expected in a study such
as this. These difficulties were discussed in Chapter III. However, a
major conclusion of this dissertation is that it is indeed feasible to

102

103

estimate simultaneously all the parameters of these types of general equilibrium models.

This research could be extended in several directions. First, the dynamic structure of the estimated model could be analyzed by finding its characteristic roots. This could be carried out using the program CONTINEST, written by Wymer (1975).

Second, the model as it now stands could be used in other interesting policy simulations, such as the effects of unemployment on the volume of trade flows, domestic prices, and the balance of trade.

A third extension could be to test some of the hypotheses which, in this study, have been treated as maintained. Imposing the overidentifying restrictions resulting from these hypotheses increases the efficiency of the estimator if they are correct, since fewer parameters have to be estimated. However, if these restrictions are not supported by the data, the result may be inconsistent estimates. These tests would require a larger sample than the one we have used.

Fourth, it would be quite straightforward to disaggregate the data base and re-estimate the model with more than three individually distinguished commodities. An application of further disaggregation could be to allow imports, or some component thereof, and domestically produced importables to be imperfect substitutes; analogously for exports and domestically consumed exportables.

A final, and more fundamental, extension would be to make the supply side of the model explicitly dynamic by introducing elements of factor specificity in the short run, along the lines developed by Mayer (1974) and Mussa (1977, 1974).

APPENDIX

THE DATA BASE

In this appendix, we set out the procedures used to construct the
U.S. data base, the primary sources of the raw data, and, finally, a list-
ing of all variables used in estimation.

Unless otherwise noted, the primary sources for all the raw data
are U.S. Department of Commerce, Office of Business Economics, The National
Income and Product Accounts of the United States, 1929-1965, Statistical
Tables, and July issues of U.S. Department of Commerce, Office of Business
Economics, Survey of Current Business. We use the convention adopted in the
text of denoting the exportables sector by the subscript 1, importables by
2, and nontraded goods by 3. All variables (except prices) are deflated
by population, and the units of all values are current dollars per capita.

For estimation of the model, the sample period is 1952 to 1971.
Here, however, we also give the values of all variables in 1951, which
represent the initial observations on the lagged variables of the model.

Output

The value of output of each sector is constructed by allocating the
components of GNP (consumption, investment, government expenditure, exports
and imports) into exportables, importables, nontraded goods and debt service.

For consumption and investment, this procedure is carried out by
classifying their components into the three sectors by attempting to match
these components with the 1971 U.S. trade data at the two and three digit

SITC level. That is, from the trade data we determine which commodities are exported and which imported in 1971, assume that this trading pattern is constant over the sample period (i.e., trade reversals are ruled out), and then apply this information to the disaggregated consumption data (81 commodities), for example, to classify total consumption expenditure into exportables and importables; consumption expenditure on nontraded goods is the residual. The source of the trade data is the OECD Statistics of Foreign Trade, Trade by Commodities: Country Summaries, Series B, No. 4, January-December, 1971.

The details of the classification of the components of consumption and investment are as follows. The following National Accounts consumption components are allocated to exportables (the National Accounts consumption component codes are in parentheses):

Half of food less tobacco (I less I.5)

Tobacco products (I.5)

Drug preparations and sundries (VI.1)

Ophthalmic products and orthopedic appliances (VI.2).

The following components are allocated to importables:

Half of food less tobacco (I less I.5)

Clothing, accessories and jewelry (II) less

Cleaning, dyeing, pressing, etc. (II.5)

Laundering (II.6)

Other (II.8)

Household operation (V) less

Household utilities (V.8)

Telephone and telegraph (V.9)

Domestic service (V.10)

Other (V.11)

New cars and net purchases of used cars (VIII.1.a)

Tires, tubes, accessories and parts (VIII.1.b)

Nondurable toys and sport supplies (IX.3)

Wheel goods, etc. (IX.4)

Radio and television receivers, etc. (IX.5)

Foreign travel and other, net (XII).

All other consumption is allocated to nontraded goods. The following
National Accounts investment components are allocated to exportables:

Total private purchases of producer durable equipment

other than passenger cars

Half the change in business inventories.

The following are allocated to importables:

Investment in passenger cars

Half the change in business inventories.

Total investment in private structures (residential and nonresi-
dential), the remaining component of total investment, is allocated to
nontraded goods.

All of government purchases of goods and services is allocated to
the nontraded goods sector.

The value of the total output of the exportables sector is obtained by adding consumption and investment expenditure on exportables to
the value of exports of goods and services, as recorded in the National
Accounts, less income on U.S. investments abroad (which is included in the
National Accounts definition of exports of goods and services). Similarly,
the value of the total output of the importables sector is obtained by
subtracting from the sum of consumption and investment expenditure on
importables the value of imports of goods and services, to which is then

added income on foreign investments in the U.S. (which is included in the National Accounts definition of imports of goods and services). The value of the total output of the nontraded goods sector is the sum of consumption and investment expenditure on nontraded goods plus total government expenditure.

We use the implicit price deflator for exports as our own measure of the domestic price of exportables, and the imports deflator for the domestic price of importables. We construct a price index for nontraded goods as the residual from the GNP implicit price deflator using the previously mentioned two indexes, and current period value of output weights. We rebase each index so that they all have a unit mean.

The output of a sector is given by deflating the value of output by its price index.

The price indexes are listed in Table 20; here, p_i is the price index for the output of sector i. We also give in this table the aggregate price index, P, the construction of which is discussed in the text.

The output series for each sector is listed in Table 21; here, z_i is an index of the output of sector i.

Consumption, Investment and Absorption

The classification of the components of consumption was discussed in the previous section. The only additional feature that requires noting here is that total government purchases of goods and services less investment in public structure is included in consumption expenditure on nontraded goods.

The consumption expenditure on each good is given in Table 22; here, v_i^c is consumption expenditure on good i. Also in this table we give total consumption expenditure C.

TABLE 20

PRICE INDEXES[a]

Year	P_1	P_2	P_3	P
1951	0.9332	1.0279	0.6398	0.7540
1952	0.9505	0.9934	0.6992	0.7913
1953	0.9160	0.9503	0.7458	0.8118
1954	0.9072	0.9666	0.7641	0.8279
1955	0.9130	0.9646	0.7796	0.8385
1956	0.9380	0.9828	0.8162	0.8698
1957	0.9746	0.9972	0.8555	0.9027
1958	0.9620	0.9589	0.9140	0.9302
1959	0.9505	0.9522	0.9451	0.9475
1960	0.9611	0.9685	0.9634	0.9647
1961	0.9804	0.9598	0.9789	0.9735
1962	0.9697	0.9444	1.0064	0.9855
1963	0.9678	0.9541	1.0255	1.0002
1964	0.9765	0.9771	1.0419	1.0180
1965	1.0053	0.9905	1.0602	1.0356
1966	1.0352	1.0116	1.0886	1.0620
1967	1.0534	0.9991	1.1371	1.0894
1968	1.0669	1.0327	1.1964	1.1372
1969	1.1025	1.0653	1.2641	1.1913
1970	1.1593	1.1373	1.3289	1.2580
1971	1.2102	1.1938	1.3893	1.3165

[a]See text for meaning of notation.

TABLE 21

OUTPUT[a]

Year	z_1	z_2	z_3
1951	535.42	511.13	1709.48
1952	502.07	501.98	1738.81
1953	506.55	537.96	1743.33
1954	496.05	517.46	1682.09
1955	545.83	584.98	1709.95
1956	574.50	558.25	1706.16
1957	575.06	550.18	1698.93
1958	539.13	549.88	1653.22
1959	584.89	611.84	1671.78
1960	601.61	608.67	1668.38
1961	581.66	604.81	1698.80
1962	624.88	660.34	1742.83
1963	647.89	681.15	1777.94
1964	690.17	703.19	1830.23
1965	723.04	749.09	1896.13
1966	793.38	772.57	1998.46
1967	785.04	773.76	2063.63
1968	819.23	811.86	2151.04
1969	843.83	834.30	2177.50
1970	852.52	779.37	2162.35
1971	831.76	799.24	2224.71

[a]See text for meaning of notation.

TABLE 22

CONSUMPTION EXPENDITURE[a]

Year	v_1^c	v_2^c	v_3^c	C
1951	241.34	568.66	848.89	1658.88
1952	250.14	571.80	964.25	1786.19
1953	250.75	593.56	1036.65	1880.95
1954	248.76	584.25	1010.63	1843.63
1955	251.64	630.61	1034.40	1916.64
1956	259.06	632.07	1083.67	1974.79
1957	269.24	645.69	1145.69	2060.62
1958	275.88	634.68	1203.08	2113.64
1959	282.51	680.23	1248.13	2210.87
1960	285.64	684.99	1289.96	2260.59
1961	289.65	679.59	1342.64	2311.88
1962	295.25	718.56	1415.70	2429.51
1963	300.77	747.76	1473.06	2521.59
1964	310.69	795.63	1544.84	2651.16
1965	326.13	851.41	1624.13	2801.67
1966	348.35	903.88	1779.37	3031.60
1967	355.52	929.75	1951.05	3236.33
1968	373.91	1019.29	2130.92	3524.12
1969	387.63	1084.27	2280.53	3752.43
1970	418.68	1115.05	2403.72	3937.45
1971	428.90	1207.91	2549.81	4186.62

[a]See text for meaning of notation.

111

The classification of the components of investment was also given in the previous section. The additional feature on the demand side is that investment in public structures (part of total government purchases of goods and services in the National Accounts) is allocated to the investment demand for nontraded goods.

The investment demand for each of the three goods is given in Table 23; here, v_i^1 is expenditure on the output of sector i for investment purposes. Also in this table, we give total investment expenditure I, and absorption A, the sum of consumption and investment.

Exports, Imports, Debt Service and the Trade Balance

The value of exports is obtained by subtracting from exports of goods and services, as recorded in the National Accounts, income on U.S. investments abroad. By construction, the value of exports is also equal to the value of domestic production of exportables less total domestic expenditure on exportables (consumption plus investment demand).

Similarly, the value of imports is obtained by subtracting from imports of goods and services income on foreign investments in the U.S. The value of imports also equals total domestic expenditure on importables less the value of domestic production of that commodity.

The surplus on the debt service account is just income on U.S. investments abroad less income on foreign investments in the U.S.

The value of exports less the value of imports is the trade balance.

In Table 24 we give the value of exports and imports, denoted by e_1 and $-e_2$, respectively, the surplus on the debt service account DS, and, finally, the trade balance B.

TABLE 23

INVESTMENT EXPENDITURE AND ABSORPTION[a]

Year	v_1^i	v_2^i	v_3^i	I	A
1951	149.05	51.52	244.91	445.48	2104.36
1952	124.11	24.63	251.54	400.28	2186.47
1953	119.02	18.52	263.51	401.05	2282.00
1954	105.62	11.42	274.61	391.66	2235.29
1955	141.68	38.35	298.69	478.71	2395.35
1956	155.38	29.90	308.85	494.13	2468.92
1957	153.07	20.37	307.72	481.16	2541.78
1958	126.63	8.56	307.90	443.08	2556.72
1959	157.96	29.46	331.90	519.33	2730.20
1960	160.36	26.98	317.37	504.71	2765.30
1961	146.57	20.29	320.36	487.22	2799.10
1962	172.19	33.83	338.19	544.21	2973.72
1963	180.07	34.72	350.25	565.04	3086.63
1964	198.90	32.07	362.12	593.09	3244.25
1965	230.65	46.31	386.17	663.14	3464.81
1966	283.00	60.11	396.19	739.29	3770.89
1967	273.12	37.33	395.43	705.89	3942.22
1968	282.45	44.30	442.66	769.42	4293.54
1969	308.78	46.88	471.95	827.61	4580.04
1970	304.66	36.11	469.87	810.64	4748.09
1971	304.19	38.94	540.92	884.05	5070.67

[a]See text for meaning of notation.

113

TABLE 24

VALUE OF EXPORTS, IMPORTS, DEBT SERVICE SURPLUS, AND TRADE BALANCE[a]

Year	e_1	$-e_2$	DS	B
1951	109.28	95.00	9.51	14.28
1952	102.96	97.74	8.96	5.22
1953	94.22	100.88	9.08	-6.66
1954	95.64	95.51	11.13	0.13
1955	105.02	104.69	11.83	0.33
1956	124.45	113.32	12.45	11.14
1957	138.14	117.41	12.71	20.72
1958	116.15	115.98	12.50	0.17
1959	115.45	127.13	12.51	-11.68
1960	132.23	122.49	12.66	9.73
1961	134.02	119.40	15.96	14.62
1962	138.51	128.74	17.71	9.77
1963	146.20	132.62	17.56	13.57
1964	164.35	140.61	20.46	23.73
1965	170.09	155.74	21.40	14.35
1966	189.95	182.43	18.27	7.52
1967	198.34	194.01	19.61	4.33
1968	217.67	225.22	19.96	-7.55
1969	233.90	242.37	17.89	-8.46
1970	264.98	264.77	17.18	0.20
1971	273.53	292.73	22.72	-19.20

[a]See text for meaning of notation.

Income, Change in Domestic
Credit, and Wealth

Income is defined as nominal GNP plus the sum of the change in the
domestic credit component of the monetary base and the change in the
nominal value of wealth due to inflation. The income variable, denoted by
Y, is listed in Table 25.

The source for the domestic credit variable is the IMF, International
Financial Statistics, 1972 Supplement. In the Monetary Authorities section
of that source, unclassified liabilities were assumed to represent the
capital of the central bank and hence were subtracted from total liabilities
to yield the quantity of high-powered money. Foreign assets were then subtracted from high-powered money to give the domestic credit component of
the monetary base. The change in this variable, ΔD, is given in Table 25.

We compute the change in the nominal value of wealth due to inflation as the product of the percentage change in the aggregate price index
and the value of the previous year's wealth, $\hat{P}W_{-1}$.

It is important to note that the whole data base is constructed in
such a way that it is internally consistent. That is, the total value of
output in all sectors (Tables 20 and 21) plus the debt service surplus
(Table 24) is identically equal to GNP ($=Y-\Delta D-\hat{P}W_{-1}$). Also, the sum of
absorption (Table 23), the trade balance (Table 24), and the debt service
surplus (Table 24) identically equals GNP. This internal consistency means
that the economy's budget constraint is satisfied at all data points.

We construct nominal wealth recursively by adding to the previous
period's wealth the difference between income (as defined above) and total
consumption expenditure (as defined above)--i.e., the stock of wealth is
increased by the economy consuming less than its income. We initialize
this procedure in 1938 by capitalizing permanent income in that year at a

TABLE 25

INCOME, CHANGE IN DOMESTIC CREDIT, AND WEALTH[a]

Year	Y	ΔD	W
1951	2608.07	20.74	13842.0
1952	2878.61	5.73	14696.3
1953	2666.82	6.27	15242.8
1954	2538.64	-4.93	15675.0
1955	2609.56	4.84	16092.9
1956	3083.48	0.59	16924.1
1957	3195.20	-7.59	17752.4
1958	3111.66	10.34	18464.9
1959	3078.20	8.47	19019.5
1960	3141.75	16.60	19521.7
1961	3009.36	4.35	19889.9
1962	3257.20	15.53	20408.7
1963	3431.58	13.73	21027.7
1964	3675.81	18.22	21756.8
1965	3893.43	20.56	22569.1
1966	4390.51	26.41	23664.4
1967	4598.06	26.62	24764.6
1968	5402.65	19.43	26445.7
1969	5847.61	12.33	28279.9
1970	6357.34	25.87	30396.2
1971	6516.82	43.00	32418.0

[a]See text for meaning of notation.

nominal interest rate of 10 percent per annum to yield an initial value of
wealth. The aim here is to use as an initial condition for wealth a year
far enough away from the beginning of the sample period so that it has a
negligible effect. Also, the aim is to use a year which, as far as possible,
is not distorted by special conditions, such as The Depression and World
War II.

We estimate permanent income in 1938 as

$$Y^P = \sum_{i=0}^{4} \omega_i Y_{-i}$$

in which the ω's are weights and Y is our measure of income, previously defined. The value of the weights are derived from Friedman (1957, Table 15,
p. 147). In particular, we use a normalized version of the first five of
his weights which were estimated in his U.S. consumption function study.
This yields the following weight vector:

$$[.382 \qquad .256 \qquad .171 \qquad .114 \qquad .077].$$

The use of only the first five of Friedman's seventeen estimated weights
should be satisfactory since they account for 86.5 percent of the total
sum of the weights.

The effects of the 1938 stock on the wealth series within the sample
period should be reasonably small. Hence, the effects of the somewhat
arbitrary way of calculating this initial stock should also be small.

For the period 1938 to 1950, two years before the commencement of
our sample period, the change in the nominal value of wealth, used in the
definition of income in the above procedure, was approximated as follows.
Instead of using the percentage change in the Divisia index in $\hat{P}W_{-1}$, as
discussed in the text, we used the proportionate change in the GNP deflator.
The error involved is likely to be small.

The wealth variable, denoted by W, is listed in Table 25.

Aggregate Factor Endowment Index

The total number of full-time equivalent employees in all industries is our aggregate factor endowment index. We denote it by K and it is listed in Table 26. Here, the units are the number of equivalent employees per capita.

TABLE 26

AGGREGATE FACTOR ENDOWMENT INDEX[a]

Year	K
1951	0.3447
1952	0.3465
1953	0.3469
1954	0.3300
1955	0.3319
1956	0.3341
1957	0.3295
1958	0.3150
1959	0.3173
1960	0.3160
1961	0.3098
1962	0.3131
1963	0.3133
1964	0.3158
1965	0.3228
1966	0.3358
1967	0.3411
1968	0.3479
1969	0.3542
1970	0.3494
1971	0.3438

[a]See text for meaning of notation.

BIBLIOGRAPHY

Arndt, H. W. "Non-traded Goods and the Balance of Payments: The Australian Contribution." *Economic Record* 52, No. 137 (March 1976):104-107.

Barten, A. P., and Geysken, E. "The Negativity Condition in Consumer Demand." *European Economic Review* 6 (1975):227-260.

Berndt, Ernst R., and Savin, N. Eugene. "Estimation and Hypothesis Testing in Singular Equation Systems with Autoregressive Disturbances." *Econometrica* 43, No. 5-6 (September/November 1975):937-957.

Betancourt, Roger R. "Household Behaviour in a Less Developed Country: An Econometric Analysis of Cross-Section Data." Department of Economics, University of Maryland, August 1973. (Mimeographed.)

Brown, Alan, and Deaton, Angus. "Surveys in Applied Economics: Models of Consumer Behavior." *Economic Journal* 82 (September 1972):1145-1236.

Christensen, Laurits R.; Jorgenson, Dale W.; and Lau, Lawrence J. "Transcendental Logarithmic Production Frontiers." *Review of Economics and Statistics* 55 (1973):28-45.

Diewert, W. E. "Functional Forms for Profit and Transformation Functions." *Journal of Economic Theory* 6 (1973):284-316.

_____. "Functional Forms for Revenue and Factor Requirements Functions *International Economic Review* 15, No. 1 (February 1974):119-130.

Dixon, Peter, and Lluch, Constantino. "Durable Goods in the Complete System Approach to Applied Demand Theory." Third World Congress of the Econometric Society, Toronto, August 1975. (Mimeographed.) Forthcoming in the *Review of Economic Studies*.

Dixon, Peter B.; Vincent, David P.; and Powell, Alan A. "Factor Demand and Product Supply Relations in Australian Agriculture: The CRESH/CRETH Production System." Impact of Demographic Change on Industry Structure in Australia, Preliminary Working Paper No. OP-08, Melbourne, Australia, November 1976. (Mimeographed.)

Dornbusch, Rudiger. "Currency Depreciation, Hoarding, and Relative Prices." *Journal of Political Economy* 81, No. 4 (July/August 1973):893-915.(a)

_____. "Devaluation, Money, and Non-traded Goods." *American Economic Review* 63 (December 1973):871-883. (b)

_____. "Real and Monetary Aspects of the Effects of Exchange Rate Chan Changes," in *National Monetary Policies and the International Financial System*. Edited by R. Z. Aliber. Chicago: University of Chicago Press, 1974. Pp. 64-81.

118

Dornbusch, Rudiger, and Mussa, Michael. "Consumption, Real Balances and the Hoarding Function." _International Economic Review_ 16, No. 2 (June 1975):415-421.

Fischer, Stanley, and Frenkel, Jacob A. "Investment, the Two-Sector Model and Trade in Debt and Capital Goods." _Journal of International Economics_ 2 (August 1972):211-233.

_____. "Economic Growth and Stages of the Balance of Payments: A Theoretical Model," in _Trade, Stability and Macroeconomics: Essays in Honor of Lloyd A. Metzler._ Edited by G. Horwich and P. A. Samuelson. New York: Academic Press, 1974. Pp. 503-521. (a)

_____. "Interest Rate Equalization, Patterns of Production, Trade and Consumption in a Two-Country Growth Model." _Economic Record_ 50 (December 1974):555-580. (b)

Frenkel, Jacob A. "A Theory of Money, Trade and the Balance of Payments in a Model of Accumulation." _Journal of International Economics_ 1 (May 1971):159-187.

Frenkel, Jacob A., and Rodriguez, Carlos A. "Portfolio Equilibrium and the Balance of Payments: A Monetary Approach." _American Economic Review_ 65, No. 4 (September 1975):674-688.

Friedman, Milton. _A Theory of the Consumption Function._ Princeton: Princeton University Press, 1957.

Goldberger, Arthur S. "Functional Form and Utility: A Review of Consumer Demand Theory." Systems Formulation, Methodology and Policy Workship Paper 6703, University of Wisconsin, October 1967.

Hall, Robert E. "The Specification of Technology with Several Kinds of Output." _Journal of Political Economy_ 81, No. 4 (July/August 1973):878-892.

Harberger, A. C. "Currency Depreciation, Income, and the Balance of Trade." _Journal of Political Economy_ 58, No. 1 (February 1950):47-60.

Hasenkamp, Georg. _Specification and Estimation of Multiple-Output Production Functions._ New York: Springer-Verlag, 1976. (a)

_____. "A Study of Multiple-Output Production Functions: Klein's Railroad Study Revisited." _Journal of Econometrics_ 4, No. 3 (August 1976):253-262. (b)

Johnson, Harry G. "The Transfer Problem and Exchange Stability." _Journal of Political Economy_ 64, No. 3 (June 1956):212-225.

_____. "Towards a General Theory of the Balance of Payments," in _International Trade and Economic Growth._ London: Allen & Unwin, 1958. Pp. 153-168.

Johnson, Harry G. "The Costs of Protection and Self-Sufficiency." *Quarterly Journal of Economics* 72, No. 3 (August 1965):356-372.

_____. *The Two-Sector Model of General Equilibrium*. Chicago: Aldine Atherton, 1971.

_____. "The Monetary Theory of Balance of Payments Policies," in *The Monetary Approach to the Balance of Payments*. Edited by Jacob A. Frenkel and Harry G. Johnson. Toronto: University of Toronto Press, 1976. Pp. 262-284. (a)

_____. "Elasticity, Absorption, Keynesian Multiplier, Keynesian Policy, and Monetary Approaches to Devaluation Theory: A Simple Geometric Exposition." *American Economic Review* 66, No. 3 (June 1976):448-452. (b)

Jones, R. W. "The Structure of Simple General Equilibrium Models." *Journal of Political Economy* 73 (December 1965):557-572.

Jonson, P. D. "Money and Economic Activity in the Open Economy: The United Kingdom, 1880-1970." *Journal of Political Economy* 84, No. 5 (October 1976):979-1012.

Jonson, P. D., and Danes, M. K. "Money and Inflation: Some Analytic Issues." Reserve Bank of Australia, Sydney, September 1976. (Mimeographed.)

Klein, L. R., and Rubin, H. "A Constant Utility Index of the Cost of Living." *Review of Economic Studies* 15, No. 2 (1947-48):84-87.

Klijn, Nico. "The Specification of the Extended Linear Expenditure System: Some Alternatives." Research School of Social Sciences, Australian National University, August 1974. (Mimeographed.)

Komiya, R. "Non-Traded Goods and the Pure Theory of International Trade." *International Economic Review* 8 (June 1967):132-152.

Lluch, Constantino. "The Extended Linear Expenditure System." *European Economic Review* 4, No. 1 (April 1973):21-32.

Lluch, Constantino, and Powell, Alan. "International Comparisons of Expenditure Patterns." *European Economic Review* 5 (1975):275-303.

Lluch, Constantino; Powell, Alan; and Williams, Ross. *Household Demand and Saving in Economic Development: Applications of Linear Demand Systems*. Forthcoming, 1977.

Lluch, Constantino, and Williams, Ross. "Consumer Demand Systems and Aggregate Consumption in the USA: An Application of the Extended Linear Expenditure System." *Canadian Journal of Economics* 8, No. 1 (February 1975):49-66.

Magee, Stephen P. "Prices, Incomes, and Foreign Trade," in _International Trade and Finance: Frontiers for Research_. Edited by Peter B. Kenen. Cambridge: Cambridge University Press, 1975. Pp. 175-252.

Mattei, Aurelio. "An Intertemporal Model of Consumer Behavior." Institute for Economic Research, Swiss Federal Institute of Technology, 1973. (Mimeographed.)

Mayer, Wolfgang. "Short-Run and Long-Run Equilibrium for a Small Open Economy." _Journal of Political Economy_ 82, No. 5 (September/October 1974):955-968.

Melvin, James R. "Production and Trade with Two Factors and Three Goods." _American Economic Review_ 58, No. 5 (December 1968):1249-1268.

Metzler, Lloyd A. "Wealth, Saving, and the Rate of Interest." _Journal of Political Economy_ 59 (April 1951):93-116.

Mundell, Robert A. _International Economics_. New York: Macmillan, 1968.

Mundlak, Yair. "Specification and Estimation of Multiproduct Production Functions." _Journal of Farm Economics_ 45, No. 2 (May 1963):433-443.

_____. "Transcendental Multiproduct Production Functions." _International Economic Review_ 5, No. 3 (September 1964):273-284.

Mussa, Michael. "Tariffs and the Distribution of Income: The Importance of Factor Specificity, Substitutability, and Intensity in the Short and Long Run." _Journal of Political Economy_ 82, No. 6 (November/December 1974):1191-1203.

_____. "Dynamic Adjustment in the Heckscher-Ohlin Samuelson Model." University of Chicago, January 1977. (Mimeographed.)

Ohlin, B. _Interregional and International Trade_. Cambridge: Harvard University Press, 1933.

Oppenheimer, P. M. "Non-traded Goods and the Balance of Payments: A Historical Note." _Journal of Economic Literature_ 12 (September 1974):882-888.

Philips, Louis. _Applied Consumption Analysis_. Amsterdam: North Holland, 1974.

Pollak, Robert A. "Subindexes of the Cost of Living Index." _International Economic Review_ 16, No. 1 (February 1975):135-150.

Pollak, Robert A., and Wales, Terence J. "Estimation of the Linear Expenditure System." _Econometrica_ 37, No. 4 (October 1969):611-628.

Powell, Alan A. "The Dynamics Behind the Linear Expenditure System." Department of Econometrics and Operations Research, Monash University, May 1974. (Mimeographed.) (a)

122

Powell, Alan A. _Empirical Analytics of Demand Systems_. Lexington, Mass.: D. C. Heath, 1974. (b)

Powell, Alan A., and Gruen, F. H. G. "The Constant Elasticity of Transformation Production Frontier and Linear Supply Systems." _International Economic Review_ 9, No. 3 (October 1968):315-28.

Prais, S. J. "Some Mathematical Notes on the Quantity Theory of Money in an Open Economy." _IMF Staff Papers_ 8, No. 2 (May 1961):212-226.

Rodriguez, Carlos A. "The Terms of Trade and the Balance of Payments in the Short Run." _American Economic Review_ 66, No. 4 (September 1976):710-716.

Sidrauski, Miguel. "Rational Choice and Patterns of Growth in a Monetary Economy." _American Economic Review: Papers and Proceedings_ 57, No. 2 (May 1967):534-544.

Sjaastad, Larry A. "On the Monetary Theory of the Balance of Payments: An Extension." Sixth Konstanz Seminar on Monetary Theory and Policy, Konstanz, Germany, June 1975. (Mimeographed.)

Stone, Richard. "Linear Expenditure Systems and Demand Analysis: An Application to the Pattern of British Demand." _Economic Journal_ 64, No. 255 (September 1954):511-527.

Theil, Henri. _Principles of Econometrics_. New York: Wiley, 1971.

Wymer, C. R. "Computer Programs: RESIMUL Manual." London School of Economics, July 1973. (Mimeographed.)

_____. "Computer Programs: PREDIC Manual." London School of Economics, May 1974. (Mimeographed.)

_____. "Computer Programs: CONTINEST Manual." London School of Economics, June 1975. (Mimeographed.)

For Product Safety Concerns and Information please contact our EU representative GPSR@taylorandfrancis.com Taylor & Francis Verlag GmbH, Kaufingerstraße 24, 80331 München, Germany